Mometrix
TEST PREPARATION

DSST Human Resource Management Exam Secrets Study Guide

DEAR FUTURE EXAM SUCCESS STORY

First of all, **THANK YOU** for purchasing Mometrix study materials!

Second, congratulations! You are one of the few determined test-takers who are committed to doing whatever it takes to excel on your exam. **You have come to the right place.** We developed these study materials with one goal in mind: to deliver you the information you need in a format that's concise and easy to use.

In addition to optimizing your guide for the content of the test, we've outlined our recommended steps for breaking down the preparation process into small, attainable goals so you can make sure you stay on track.

We've also analyzed the entire test-taking process, identifying the most common pitfalls and showing how you can overcome them and be ready for any curveball the test throws you.

Standardized testing is one of the biggest obstacles on your road to success, which only increases the importance of doing well in the high-pressure, high-stakes environment of test day. Your results on this test could have a significant impact on your future, and this guide provides the information and practical advice to help you achieve your full potential on test day.

Your success is our success

We would love to hear from you! If you would like to share the story of your exam success or if you have any questions or comments in regard to our products, please contact us at **800-673-8175** or **support@mometrix.com**.

Thanks again for your business and we wish you continued success!

Sincerely,
The Mometrix Test Preparation Team

Need more help? Check out our flashcards at:
http://MometrixFlashcards.com/DSST

Written and edited by the Mometrix Exam Secrets Test Prep Team
Printed in the United States of America

TABLE OF CONTENTS

Introduction

Thank you for purchasing this resource! You have made the choice to prepare yourself for a test that could have a huge impact on your future, and this guide is designed to help you be fully ready for test day. Obviously, it's important to have a solid understanding of the test material, but you also need to be prepared for the unique environment and stressors of the test, so that you can perform to the best of your abilities.

For this purpose, the first section that appears in this guide is the **Secret Keys**. We've devoted countless hours to meticulously researching what works and what doesn't, and we've boiled down our findings to the five most impactful steps you can take to improve your performance on the test. We start at the beginning with study planning and move through the preparation process, all the way to the testing strategies that will help you get the most out of what you know when you're finally sitting in front of the test.

We recommend that you start preparing for your test as far in advance as possible. However, if you've bought this guide as a last-minute study resource and only have a few days before your test, we recommend that you skip over the first two Secret Keys since they address a long-term study plan.

If you struggle with **test anxiety**, we strongly encourage you to check out our recommendations for how you can overcome it. Test anxiety is a formidable foe, but it can be beaten, and we want to make sure you have the tools you need to defeat it.

Secret Key #1 – Plan Big, Study Small

There's a lot riding on your performance. If you want to ace this test, you're going to need to keep your skills sharp and the material fresh in your mind. You need a plan that lets you review everything you need to know while still fitting in your schedule. We'll break this strategy down into three categories.

Information Organization

Start with the information you already have: the official test outline. From this, you can make a complete list of all the concepts you need to cover before the test. Organize these concepts into groups that can be studied together, and create a list of any related vocabulary you need to learn so you can brush up on any difficult terms. You'll want to keep this vocabulary list handy once you actually start studying since you may need to add to it along the way.

Time Management

Once you have your set of study concepts, decide how to spread them out over the time you have left before the test. Break your study plan into small, clear goals so you have a manageable task for each day and know exactly what you're doing. Then just focus on one small step at a time. When you manage your time this way, you don't need to spend hours at a time studying. Studying a small block of content for a short period each day helps you retain information better and avoid stressing over how much you have left to do. You can relax knowing that you have a plan to cover everything in time. In order for this strategy to be effective though, you have to start studying early and stick to your schedule. Avoid the exhaustion and futility that comes from last-minute cramming!

Study Environment

The environment you study in has a big impact on your learning. Studying in a coffee shop, while probably more enjoyable, is not likely to be as fruitful as studying in a quiet room. It's important to keep distractions to a minimum. You're only planning to study for a short block of time, so make the most of it. Don't pause to check your phone or get up to find a snack. It's also important to **avoid multitasking**. Research has consistently shown that multitasking will make your studying dramatically less effective. Your study area should also be comfortable and well-lit so you don't have the distraction of straining your eyes or sitting on an uncomfortable chair.

The time of day you study is also important. You want to be rested and alert. Don't wait until just before bedtime. Study when you'll be most likely to comprehend and remember. Even better, if you know what time of day your test will be, set that time aside for study. That way your brain will be used to working on that subject at that specific time and you'll have a better chance of recalling information.

Finally, it can be helpful to team up with others who are studying for the same test. Your actual studying should be done in as isolated an environment as possible, but the work of organizing the information and setting up the study plan can be divided up. In between study sessions, you can discuss with your teammates the concepts that you're all studying and quiz each other on the details. Just be sure that your teammates are as serious about the test as you are. If you find that your study time is being replaced with social time, you might need to find a new team.

Secret Key #2 – Make Your Studying Count

You're devoting a lot of time and effort to preparing for this test, so you want to be absolutely certain it will pay off. This means doing more than just reading the content and hoping you can remember it on test day. It's important to make every minute of study count. There are two main areas you can focus on to make your studying count.

Retention

It doesn't matter how much time you study if you can't remember the material. You need to make sure you are retaining the concepts. To check your retention of the information you're learning, try recalling it at later times with minimal prompting. Try carrying around flashcards and glance at one or two from time to time or ask a friend who's also studying for the test to quiz you.

To enhance your retention, look for ways to put the information into practice so that you can apply it rather than simply recalling it. If you're using the information in practical ways, it will be much easier to remember. Similarly, it helps to solidify a concept in your mind if you're not only reading it to yourself but also explaining it to someone else. Ask a friend to let you teach them about a concept you're a little shaky on (or speak aloud to an imaginary audience if necessary). As you try to summarize, define, give examples, and answer your friend's questions, you'll understand the concepts better and they will stay with you longer. Finally, step back for a big picture view and ask yourself how each piece of information fits with the whole subject. When you link the different concepts together and see them working together as a whole, it's easier to remember the individual components.

Finally, practice showing your work on any multi-step problems, even if you're just studying. Writing out each step you take to solve a problem will help solidify the process in your mind, and you'll be more likely to remember it during the test.

Modality

Modality simply refers to the means or method by which you study. Choosing a study modality that fits your own individual learning style is crucial. No two people learn best in exactly the same way, so it's important to know your strengths and use them to your advantage.

For example, if you learn best by visualization, focus on visualizing a concept in your mind and draw an image or a diagram. Try color-coding your notes, illustrating them, or creating symbols that will trigger your mind to recall a learned concept. If you learn best by hearing or discussing information, find a study partner who learns the same way or read aloud to yourself. Think about how to put the information in your own words. Imagine that you are giving a lecture on the topic and record yourself so you can listen to it later.

For any learning style, flashcards can be helpful. Organize the information so you can take advantage of spare moments to review. Underline key words or phrases. Use different colors for different categories. Mnemonic devices (such as creating a short list in which every item starts with the same letter) can also help with retention. Find what works best for you and use it to store the information in your mind most effectively and easily.

Secret Key #3 – Practice the Right Way

Your success on test day depends not only on how many hours you put into preparing, but also on whether you prepared the right way. It's good to check along the way to see if your studying is paying off. One of the most effective ways to do this is by taking practice tests to evaluate your progress. Practice tests are useful because they show exactly where you need to improve. Every time you take a practice test, pay special attention to these three groups of questions:

- The questions you got wrong
- The questions you had to guess on, even if you guessed right
- The questions you found difficult or slow to work through

This will show you exactly what your weak areas are, and where you need to devote more study time. Ask yourself why each of these questions gave you trouble. Was it because you didn't understand the material? Was it because you didn't remember the vocabulary? Do you need more repetitions on this type of question to build speed and confidence? Dig into those questions and figure out how you can strengthen your weak areas as you go back to review the material.

Additionally, many practice tests have a section explaining the answer choices. It can be tempting to read the explanation and think that you now have a good understanding of the concept. However, an explanation likely only covers part of the question's broader context. Even if the explanation makes perfect sense, **go back and investigate** every concept related to the question until you're positive you have a thorough understanding.

As you go along, keep in mind that the practice test is just that: practice. Memorizing these questions and answers will not be very helpful on the actual test because it is unlikely to have any of the same exact questions. If you only know the right answers to the sample questions, you won't be prepared for the real thing. **Study the concepts** until you understand them fully, and then you'll be able to answer any question that shows up on the test.

It's important to wait on the practice tests until you're ready. If you take a test on your first day of study, you may be overwhelmed by the amount of material covered and how much you need to learn. Work up to it gradually.

On test day, you'll need to be prepared for answering questions, managing your time, and using the test-taking strategies you've learned. It's a lot to balance, like a mental marathon that will have a big impact on your future. Like training for a marathon, you'll need to start slowly and work your way up. When test day arrives, you'll be ready.

Start with the strategies you've read in the first two Secret Keys—plan your course and study in the way that works best for you. If you have time, consider using multiple study resources to get different approaches to the same concepts. It can be helpful to see difficult concepts from more than one angle. Then find a good source for practice tests. Many times, the test website will suggest potential study resources or provide sample tests.

Practice Test Strategy

If you're able to find at least three practice tests, we recommend this strategy:

Untimed and Open-Book Practice

Take the first test with no time constraints and with your notes and study guide handy. Take your time and focus on applying the strategies you've learned.

Timed and Open-Book Practice

Take the second practice test open-book as well, but set a timer and practice pacing yourself to finish in time.

Timed and Closed-Book Practice

Take any other practice tests as if it were test day. Set a timer and put away your study materials. Sit at a table or desk in a quiet room, imagine yourself at the testing center, and answer questions as quickly and accurately as possible.

Keep repeating timed and closed-book tests on a regular basis until you run out of practice tests or it's time for the actual test. Your mind will be ready for the schedule and stress of test day, and you'll be able to focus on recalling the material you've learned.

Secret Key #4 – Pace Yourself

Once you're fully prepared for the material on the test, your biggest challenge on test day will be managing your time. Just knowing that the clock is ticking can make you panic even if you have plenty of time left. Work on pacing yourself so you can build confidence against the time constraints of the exam. Pacing is a difficult skill to master, especially in a high-pressure environment, so **practice is vital**.

Set time expectations for your pace based on how much time is available. For example, if a section has 60 questions and the time limit is 30 minutes, you know you have to average 30 seconds or less per question in order to answer them all. Although 30 seconds is the hard limit, set 25 seconds per question as your goal, so you reserve extra time to spend on harder questions. When you budget extra time for the harder questions, you no longer have any reason to stress when those questions take longer to answer.

Don't let this time expectation distract you from working through the test at a calm, steady pace, but keep it in mind so you don't spend too much time on any one question. Recognize that taking extra time on one question you don't understand may keep you from answering two that you do understand later in the test. If your time limit for a question is up and you're still not sure of the answer, mark it and move on, and come back to it later if the time and the test format allow. If the testing format doesn't allow you to return to earlier questions, just make an educated guess; then put it out of your mind and move on.

On the easier questions, be careful not to rush. It may seem wise to hurry through them so you have more time for the challenging ones, but it's not worth missing one if you know the concept and just didn't take the time to read the question fully. Work efficiently but make sure you understand the question and have looked at all of the answer choices, since more than one may seem right at first.

Even if you're paying attention to the time, you may find yourself a little behind at some point. You should speed up to get back on track, but do so wisely. Don't panic; just take a few seconds less on each question until you're caught up. Don't guess without thinking, but do look through the answer choices and eliminate any you know are wrong. If you can get down to two choices, it is often worthwhile to guess from those. Once you've chosen an answer, move on and don't dwell on any that you skipped or had to hurry through. If a question was taking too long, chances are it was one of the harder ones, so you weren't as likely to get it right anyway.

On the other hand, if you find yourself getting ahead of schedule, it may be beneficial to slow down a little. The more quickly you work, the more likely you are to make a careless mistake that will affect your score. You've budgeted time for each question, so don't be afraid to spend that time. Practice an efficient but careful pace to get the most out of the time you have.

Secret Key #5 – Have a Plan for Guessing

When you're taking the test, you may find yourself stuck on a question. Some of the answer choices seem better than others, but you don't see the one answer choice that is obviously correct. What do you do?

The scenario described above is very common, yet most test takers have not effectively prepared for it. Developing and practicing a plan for guessing may be one of the single most effective uses of your time as you get ready for the exam.

In developing your plan for guessing, there are three questions to address:

- When should you start the guessing process?
- How should you narrow down the choices?
- Which answer should you choose?

When to Start the Guessing Process

Unless your plan for guessing is to select C every time (which, despite its merits, is not what we recommend), you need to leave yourself enough time to apply your answer elimination strategies. Since you have a limited amount of time for each question, that means that if you're going to give yourself the best shot at guessing correctly, you have to decide quickly whether or not you will guess.

Of course, the best-case scenario is that you don't have to guess at all, so first, see if you can answer the question based on your knowledge of the subject and basic reasoning skills. Focus on the key words in the question and try to jog your memory of related topics. Give yourself a chance to bring the knowledge to mind, but once you realize that you don't have (or you can't access) the knowledge you need to answer the question, it's time to start the guessing process.

It's almost always better to start the guessing process too early than too late. It only takes a few seconds to remember something and answer the question from knowledge. Carefully eliminating wrong answer choices takes longer. Plus, going through the process of eliminating answer choices can actually help jog your memory.

Summary: Start the guessing process as soon as you decide that you can't answer the question based on your knowledge.

How to Narrow Down the Choices

The next chapter in this book (**Test-Taking Strategies**) includes a wide range of strategies for how to approach questions and how to look for answer choices to eliminate. You will definitely want to read those carefully, practice them, and figure out which ones work best for you. Here though, we're going to address a mindset rather than a particular strategy.

Your odds of guessing an answer correctly depend on how many options you are choosing from.

Number of options left	5	4	3	2	1
Odds of guessing correctly	20%	25%	33%	50%	100%

You can see from this chart just how valuable it is to be able to eliminate incorrect answers and make an educated guess, but there are two things that many test takers do that cause them to miss out on the benefits of guessing:

- Accidentally eliminating the correct answer
- Selecting an answer based on an impression

We'll look at the first one here, and the second one in the next section.

To avoid accidentally eliminating the correct answer, we recommend a thought exercise called **the $5 challenge**. In this challenge, you only eliminate an answer choice from contention if you are willing to bet $5 on it being wrong. Why $5? Five dollars is a small but not insignificant amount of money. It's an amount you could afford to lose but wouldn't want to throw away. And while losing $5 once might not hurt too much, doing it twenty times will set you back $100. In the same way, each small decision you make—eliminating a choice here, guessing on a question there—won't by itself impact your score very much, but when you put them all together, they can make a big difference. By holding each answer choice elimination decision to a higher standard, you can reduce the risk of accidentally eliminating the correct answer.

The $5 challenge can also be applied in a positive sense: If you are willing to bet $5 that an answer choice *is* correct, go ahead and mark it as correct.

Summary: Only eliminate an answer choice if you are willing to bet $5 that it is wrong.

Which Answer to Choose

You're taking the test. You've run into a hard question and decided you'll have to guess. You've eliminated all the answer choices you're willing to bet $5 on. Now you have to pick an answer. Why do we even need to talk about this? Why can't you just pick whichever one you feel like when the time comes?

The answer to these questions is that if you don't come into the test with a plan, you'll rely on your impression to select an answer choice, and if you do that, you risk falling into a trap. The test writers know that everyone who takes their test will be guessing on some of the questions, so they intentionally write wrong answer choices to seem plausible. You still have to pick an answer though, and if the wrong answer choices are designed to look right, how can you ever be sure that you're not falling for their trap? The best solution we've found to this dilemma is to take the decision out of your hands entirely. Here is the process we recommend:

Once you've eliminated any choices that you are confident (willing to bet $5) are wrong, select the first remaining choice as your answer.

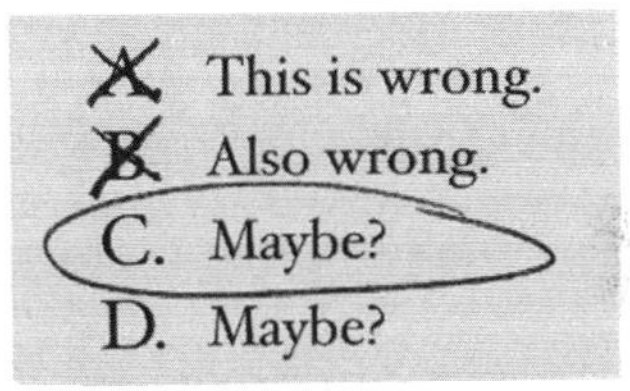

Whether you choose to select the first remaining choice, the second, or the last, the important thing is that you use some preselected standard. Using this approach guarantees that you will not be enticed into selecting an answer choice that looks right, because you are not basing your decision on how the answer choices look.

This is not meant to make you question your knowledge. Instead, it is to help you recognize the difference between your knowledge and your impressions. There's a huge difference between thinking an answer is right because of what you know, and thinking an answer is right because it looks or sounds like it should be right.

Summary: To ensure that your selection is appropriately random, make a predetermined selection from among all answer choices you have not eliminated.

Test-Taking Strategies

This section contains a list of test-taking strategies that you may find helpful as you work through the test. By taking what you know and applying logical thought, you can maximize your chances of answering any question correctly!

It is very important to realize that every question is different and every person is different: no single strategy will work on every question, and no single strategy will work for every person. That's why we've included all of them here, so you can try them out and determine which ones work best for different types of questions and which ones work best for you.

Question Strategies

☑ Read Carefully

Read the question and the answer choices carefully. Don't miss the question because you misread the terms. You have plenty of time to read each question thoroughly and make sure you understand what is being asked. Yet a happy medium must be attained, so don't waste too much time. You must read carefully and efficiently.

☑ Contextual Clues

Look for contextual clues. If the question includes a word you are not familiar with, look at the immediate context for some indication of what the word might mean. Contextual clues can often give you all the information you need to decipher the meaning of an unfamiliar word. Even if you can't determine the meaning, you may be able to narrow down the possibilities enough to make a solid guess at the answer to the question.

☑ Prefixes

If you're having trouble with a word in the question or answer choices, try dissecting it. Take advantage of every clue that the word might include. Prefixes can be a huge help. Usually, they allow you to determine a basic meaning. *Pre-* means before, *post-* means after, *pro-* is positive, *de-* is negative. From prefixes, you can get an idea of the general meaning of the word and try to put it into context.

☑ Hedge Words

Watch out for critical hedge words, such as *likely, may, can, often, almost, mostly, usually, generally, rarely,* and *sometimes.* Question writers insert these hedge phrases to cover every possibility. Often an answer choice will be wrong simply because it leaves no room for exception. Be on guard for answer choices that have definitive words such as *exactly* and *always.*

☑ Switchback Words

Stay alert for *switchbacks.* These are the words and phrases frequently used to alert you to shifts in thought. The most common switchback words are *but, although,* and *however.* Others include *nevertheless, on the other hand, even though, while, in spite of, despite,* and *regardless of.* Switchback words are important to catch because they can change the direction of the question or an answer choice.

⊘ Face Value

When in doubt, use common sense. Accept the situation in the problem at face value. Don't read too much into it. These problems will not require you to make wild assumptions. If you have to go beyond creativity and warp time or space in order to have an answer choice fit the question, then you should move on and consider the other answer choices. These are normal problems rooted in reality. The applicable relationship or explanation may not be readily apparent, but it is there for you to figure out. Use your common sense to interpret anything that isn't clear.

Answer Choice Strategies

⊘ Answer Selection

The most thorough way to pick an answer choice is to identify and eliminate wrong answers until only one is left, then confirm it is the correct answer. Sometimes an answer choice may immediately seem right, but be careful. The test writers will usually put more than one reasonable answer choice on each question, so take a second to read all of them and make sure that the other choices are not equally obvious. As long as you have time left, it is better to read every answer choice than to pick the first one that looks right without checking the others.

⊘ Answer Choice Families

An answer choice family consists of two (in rare cases, three) answer choices that are very similar in construction and cannot all be true at the same time. If you see two answer choices that are direct opposites or parallels, one of them is usually the correct answer. For instance, if one answer choice says that quantity x increases and another either says that quantity x decreases (opposite) or says that quantity y increases (parallel), then those answer choices would fall into the same family. An answer choice that doesn't match the construction of the answer choice family is more likely to be incorrect. Most questions will not have answer choice families, but when they do appear, you should be prepared to recognize them.

⊘ Eliminate Answers

Eliminate answer choices as soon as you realize they are wrong, but make sure you consider all possibilities. If you are eliminating answer choices and realize that the last one you are left with is also wrong, don't panic. Start over and consider each choice again. There may be something you missed the first time that you will realize on the second pass.

⊘ Avoid Fact Traps

Don't be distracted by an answer choice that is factually true but doesn't answer the question. You are looking for the choice that answers the question. Stay focused on what the question is asking for so you don't accidentally pick an answer that is true but incorrect. Always go back to the question and make sure the answer choice you've selected actually answers the question and is not merely a true statement.

⊘ Extreme Statements

In general, you should avoid answers that put forth extreme actions as standard practice or proclaim controversial ideas as established fact. An answer choice that states the "process should be used in certain situations, if..." is much more likely to be correct than one that states the "process should be discontinued completely." The first is a calm rational statement and doesn't even make a definitive, uncompromising stance, using a hedge word *if* to provide wiggle room, whereas the second choice is far more extreme.

⊘ BENCHMARK

As you read through the answer choices and you come across one that seems to answer the question well, mentally select that answer choice. This is not your final answer, but it's the one that will help you evaluate the other answer choices. The one that you selected is your benchmark or standard for judging each of the other answer choices. Every other answer choice must be compared to your benchmark. That choice is correct until proven otherwise by another answer choice beating it. If you find a better answer, then that one becomes your new benchmark. Once you've decided that no other choice answers the question as well as your benchmark, you have your final answer.

⊘ PREDICT THE ANSWER

Before you even start looking at the answer choices, it is often best to try to predict the answer. When you come up with the answer on your own, it is easier to avoid distractions and traps because you will know exactly what to look for. The right answer choice is unlikely to be word-for-word what you came up with, but it should be a close match. Even if you are confident that you have the right answer, you should still take the time to read each option before moving on.

General Strategies

⊘ TOUGH QUESTIONS

If you are stumped on a problem or it appears too hard or too difficult, don't waste time. Move on! Remember though, if you can quickly check for obviously incorrect answer choices, your chances of guessing correctly are greatly improved. Before you completely give up, at least try to knock out a couple of possible answers. Eliminate what you can and then guess at the remaining answer choices before moving on.

⊘ CHECK YOUR WORK

Since you will probably not know every term listed and the answer to every question, it is important that you get credit for the ones that you do know. Don't miss any questions through careless mistakes. If at all possible, try to take a second to look back over your answer selection and make sure you've selected the correct answer choice and haven't made a costly careless mistake (such as marking an answer choice that you didn't mean to mark). This quick double check should more than pay for itself in caught mistakes for the time it costs.

⊘ PACE YOURSELF

It's easy to be overwhelmed when you're looking at a page full of questions; your mind is confused and full of random thoughts, and the clock is ticking down faster than you would like. Calm down and maintain the pace that you have set for yourself. Especially as you get down to the last few minutes of the test, don't let the small numbers on the clock make you panic. As long as you are on track by monitoring your pace, you are guaranteed to have time for each question.

⊘ DON'T RUSH

It is very easy to make errors when you are in a hurry. Maintaining a fast pace in answering questions is pointless if it makes you miss questions that you would have gotten right otherwise. Test writers like to include distracting information and wrong answers that seem right. Taking a little extra time to avoid careless mistakes can make all the difference in your test score. Find a pace that allows you to be confident in the answers that you select.

⊘ KEEP MOVING

Panicking will not help you pass the test, so do your best to stay calm and keep moving. Taking deep breaths and going through the answer elimination steps you practiced can help to break through a stress barrier and keep your pace.

Final Notes

The combination of a solid foundation of content knowledge and the confidence that comes from practicing your plan for applying that knowledge is the key to maximizing your performance on test day. As your foundation of content knowledge is built up and strengthened, you'll find that the strategies included in this chapter become more and more effective in helping you quickly sift through the distractions and traps of the test to isolate the correct answer.

Now that you're preparing to move forward into the test content chapters of this book, be sure to keep your goal in mind. As you read, think about how you will be able to apply this information on the test. If you've already seen sample questions for the test and you have an idea of the question format and style, try to come up with questions of your own that you can answer based on what you're reading. This will give you valuable practice applying your knowledge in the same ways you can expect to on test day.

Good luck and good studying!

An Overview of Human Resources Management Field

Human Resources Department

In the 1800s, companies began to become larger, requiring larger numbers of workers. At the same time, working conditions were harsh and worker turnover was high. The task of hiring workers usually fell to managers, but as this job became larger and more time-consuming, companies began to develop separate departments to handle hiring as well as workforce management. These departments eventually evolved into the human resources department.

During the same time period, research into psychology and behavior led many companies and organizations to work harder to fit individuals to the work and positions for which they were best suited. This, too, became one of the tasks of the human resources department. Managers began applying ideas on human personality and motivation and their relationship to performance, to improve job satisfaction and productivity.

Personnel Management Departments

The early departments that hired workers and managed personnel were called personnel departments. The work they did was referred to as personnel management. The hiring part of their duties focused on operating employees, sales clerks and unskilled labor, but they did not participate in hiring managers or higher level employees. They also ensured employees received their paychecks and any other job benefits. After the Second World War, personnel departments began to work harder at matching workers with the most appropriate jobs, based on their skills and interests, using an approach pioneered by the military during the war. Personnel managers were not considered skilled or valued workers, and the personnel management department was not considered an important part of the company.

Government Regulation

An increase in government regulation of the workplace led personnel departments to take on larger tasks and, eventually, to gain greater respect within companies. The Civil Rights Act of 1964 in particular increased the role of personnel managers, because it fell to them to ensure hiring practices complied with the requirements of the new laws. Other, earlier laws such as the Norris-LaGuardia Act and government regulations regarding the length of the workday, minimum wage and child labor also affected the role of the personnel department. Today, a major function of the human resource department is to ensure the company is in compliance with all government regulations regarding hiring, firing and employee compensation.

Human Resource Manager

The four main functions of the human resource manager are:

1. Administration. A major part of the HR department's everyday work is administrative. This includes hiring and firing, testing job applicants, training employees and managing complaints.
2. Policy creation and implementation. In conjunction with management, HR managers help create policies and determine how they are to be implemented.

3. Employee counseling. HR managers help create and manage programs to assist with personal growth and career development and work with individual employees to help them develop a career path.
4. Employee advocate. The HR department handles complaints from employees, including sexual harassment, company policy violations or other such issues.

HR managers today must have a wide range of knowledge in order to effectively perform their duties. Among other things, they must be educated in:

- Government policies and regulations regarding business practices.
- Company policies, practices and regulations.
- Change management approaches.
- Employee management.
- Labor relations.

The HR department acts as a central repository of information about company policies and practices, hiring, training, career development, benefits, employee management and behavior, and any issues regarding relationships between the company and its employees. All departments and organizations within the company are dependent upon the HR department to ensure smooth operation.

Human Resources Functions in Small and Large Companies

HR functions are necessary for all companies, regardless of size. However, small companies often do not have enough money or personnel to establish a separate HR department. In these cases, HR issues are usually dealt with by a manager or owner. Some functions, especially financial functions such as benefits and payroll, are often outsourced in a smaller company. By contract, larger companies usually have an extensive HR department. Very large companies might even have separate departments within the main HR organization. A larger company is also subject to more stringent laws and regulations regarding employee management, and its HR department must ensure the company is in compliance.

Society for Human Resource Management (SHRM)

As the HR department's role has increased, organizations have developed that supply education and certification for those pursuing a career in HR. The largest of these is the Society for Human Resource Management (SHRM). Their professional journals help HR managers stay informed about changes and developments in the HR field. They also provide workshops and conferences for continuing education in HR. The Human Resource Certification Institute (HRCI), created by SHRM, provides two accreditation levels based on an individual's education and experience. The first level, Professional in Human Resources, requires four years of HR experience and successful completion of the organization's examination. Senior Professionals in Human Resource Management must have eight years of experience, with three of those years at a senior executive level.

Motivation

One of the roles of the HR department is to provide motivation for employees. Motivated employees have been shown to be considerably more productive than non-motivated workers. Sources of motivation for employees include:

- Money.
- Job security.
- Job satisfaction.

- Ongoing on-the-job education.
- Challenging work.

The HR department works to ensure that company policies and ways of doing business help provide the motivation individual employees need to remain happy and productive in their jobs. This could include helping employees develop a career path, recommending pay raises, or organizing company-wide morale-boosting activities

Communication

Communication is key to the smooth operation of any organization. Communication between supervisors and employees ensures employees are meeting the company goals, and that they are able to speak to supervisors about problems or questions as they go about their day-to-day work. A human resources manager must be certain that the HR policies and procedures are effectively communicated to all personnel, including managers and supervisors. They often must assist in cases where communication has not been clear and goals are misunderstood or not being met. The human resources department might even recommend or sponsor workshops or training in effective communication to help the company run more smoothly. Other training sessions might be aimed specifically at communicating specific policies, procedures or a variety of information about the company.

Leadership

Leadership has a cascading effect on every employee. If leadership is weak, tyrannical or does not empower individuals within the company, employees are not likely to work at their highest ability. Turnover in a company with ineffective leadership is typically high, with some of the most promising employees leaving for positions where they feel more appreciated and in control.

Even effective leadership comes in different styles. Some styles are better suited to some employees than others. A leadership style that does not appeal to an individual might lead that individual to leave the company. A human resources manager can serve as a mediator between an employee and their manager to help improve the situation.

Corporate Culture and Actual Practice

In any company, employees are aware of corporate mission statements and how they relate to the way a company actually treats its employees. An example might be a case where law requires that the company hire a certain number of minorities, and the company's mission statement states that they are an equal opportunity employer, but longstanding corporate culture prevents minority employees from having equal access to promotions or career development. The human resource manager must take the responsibility to ensure that the policies stated by the company's mission statements, or company policies regulated by the government, align with the way the company actually operates.

Laws Regarding Employee Treatment

An important responsibility of the human resource manager is to be aware of legal issues that affect the company, and to implement applicable laws and regulations. The HR manager must also be aware of the company's mission statement, culture, and ethical codes. These internal regulations, whether formally expressed or not, can also affect how policies are carried out. The HR manager is sometimes faced with legal issues that do not align with company values. In these cases, the manager must determine what is ethically right when making decisions about how to implement these laws or guidelines.

Human Resource Planning

Staffing Strategy

The staffing strategy determines how employees are found, recruited, hired and placed in specific positions within the company. The basic elements of the staffing strategy include:

- Planning.
- Recruiting.
- Selection.
- Placement.

The human resources department will typically have a plan in place to handle all aspects of the staffing process. Planning takes into account company growth as well as typical turnover rates to determine the number of employees that will need to be hired over time. Recruiting focuses on advertising, job fairs, and other ways to bring the company's hiring needs to the attention of qualified candidates. Through the selection and placement process, the human resources department determines which candidates best fit the company's needs, and which jobs are most suitable for individual candidates.

Human Resources Strategies

Human resources strategies must work in tandem with the company's business strategies.

Growth Strategy

Focuses on company growth. For HR, this means finding and training sufficient personnel to support this growth. Growth through mergers requires HR to manage duplicate jobs which often result in layoffs or transfers.

Turnaround Strategy

This strategy (also known as retrenchment) occurs when existing operations are not achieving desired goals. HR must often manage downsizing, including severance packages and outplacement.

Stability Strategy

The company maintains a status quo. HR's function is to retain employees. However, career growth and raises are rare in a stability strategy.

Diversification

A company decides to manage a variety of businesses. HR is often decentralized for each branch of the company, and these HR departments must coordinate with each other to positively affect overall corporate strategy.

Differentiation Strategy

The company seeks to make their products or services stand out from the competition. HR typically looks for extremely effective, skilled employees and provides extensive training and incentives for exemplary work.

Cost Leadership Strategy

The company focuses on having the lowest prices in the market. HR focuses on efficiency and productivity. These companies often hire less skilled workers and experience high turnover.

Focus Strategy

The company targets a niche market such as a specific area or a specific part of the overall population (women or minorities, for example). In these cases, HR needs to ensure that employees are a part of, or intimately understand the target market.

Human Resources Development Strategy

The human resources department's development strategy focuses on existing employees. The major components of a development strategy are:

- Managing employee performance.
- Employee training.
- Employee development.
- Career planning.

The goal of this strategy is to ensure that employees meet basic requirements in the performance of their jobs, receive training necessary to properly do their work, are continuously developing new skills and knowledge, and are working toward career goals that meet their individual needs as well as the needs of the company.

Human Resources Compensation Strategy

The compensation strategy determines how employees are compensated for their work for the company. The major elements are:

- Wages and salaries.
- Benefits.
- Employee incentives.

A defined structure for wages and salary for hourly and salaried workers provides guidelines for the amount an employee will make for a specific job. Benefits include insurance, retirement plans, workers' compensation and other compensation not directly related to salary. Some benefits are required by law, while others are determined by the individual company. Incentives can include bonuses, health incentives, day care, or other perquisites the company may choose to provide for its employees.

Organization Design

Organization design is the specific structure of jobs in an organization and how they relate and report to each other. The way a company is structured determines how the HR department functions. Some examples are:

- Functional design. A traditional structure with defined departments. There is usually one HR department that coordinates with the various departments.
- Conglomerate. The company is made up of a variety of unrelated businesses. This organization model often has a corporate HR department as well as separate departments for each business type.
- Divisional. Similar to a conglomerate, but the individual divisions are related. HR often works at a corporate level to coordinate the separate businesses.

Corporate Culture

Corporate culture is defined as a company's set of values. These values reflect what the company stands for, what it sees as important, and how it goes about its daily functions. While difficult to quantify, it has a strong effect on how employees see themselves and their employers, as well as how consumers see the company.

The human resources department must consider the corporate culture when choosing new employees. If an employee is skilled but does not reflect the corporate culture, he might not be a good fit. HR also works to train new employees on specifics of corporate culture to help them better integrate into the company and better represent the company to consumers.

Unions

In some industries, employees are represented by a union, such as the Teamsters union or the AFL-CIO. Union involvement changes the way the human resources department deals with employees. Unions enforce specific wages and work environments to protect employees and ensure they make a living wage. Although union membership has decreased in the US, many HR managers must still learn about and implement labor relations, which is the process of managing employees represented by a union.

Job Analysis

Job analysis involves gathering data about specific jobs in an organization and presenting this data to managers. Managers then use this information to determine how the jobs can be performed more efficiently, as well as to gain an understanding of what skills the jobs require. Human resource managers use this information in the process of job selection. By understanding how a job functions and how it is best performed, the HR manager can determine which candidates are best suited to a specific position. When HR managers plan how to staff and maintain sufficient personnel for a specific department, job analysis also serves as a building block in the planning process.

Job analysis typically occurs in three stages:

- Deciding what information is needed. The reason for the job analysis will determine what type of information is needed. Time and money constraints may also play a factor in this decision. Data could include job activities, equipment used, the job's context in the organization, as well as a typical schedule, required skills, and required education.
- Deciding how to collect that information. Typical methods include observation, interviews, or questionnaires.
- Deciding who will collect that information. This step often involves managers who supervise the specific job, human resources personnel, and possibly a job analyst who is a specialist hired specifically for this function.

Collecting Job Analysis Information

A basic method of job analysis is to begin by determining the knowledge, skills and abilities (KSAs) the job requires. This can lead to jobs being grouped into job families, or jobs that require similar KSAs. The KSAs and other information about the job are usually collected in one of three ways:

- Observation. An individual, usually a manager or a human resources representative, watches workers and takes notes on their basic job functions and how the job is performed.
- Interviews. Those currently performing the job are interviewed about their job functions, requirements, and skills.
- Questionnaires and checklists. These ask specific questions about the job and provide checklists where an employee can indicate what skills or abilities are needed for a particular job.

Job Analysis Techniques

The most common job analysis technique is narrative job analysis. A subject matter expert (SME) chosen by the company writes up a description of the job. Without specific guidelines or formatting requirements, these analyses can be difficult to quantify or compare.

The Fleishman job analysis system provides a taxonomy of 52 abilities. The SME determines the extent to which each ability is required for the job being analyzed.

In a task analysis inventory, the SME makes a list of all the tasks required by a job. The job analyst then determines the importance of each task, how long is usually spent on the task, and how much training is necessary to do the task

Functional analysis breaks a job description down based on how an employee interacts with people, data and things. It is not widely used outside the US Department of Labor.

The Position Analysis Questionnaire (PAQ) consists of 194 separate items divided into six sections representing work behavior, conditions, and characteristics of an individual job. It is commonly used by a number of large corporations.

The Management Position Description Questionnaire (MPDQ) is similar to the PAQ, but focuses more on managerial positions. It is used both to classify these types of jobs and to determine appropriate compensation.

The critical incidents approach focuses on specific behaviors that determine whether a job is performed effectively. If these behaviors are performed properly, the job can be said to have been done effectively. It is most widely used to develop appraisal tools.

O*NET

The Occupational Information Network, also known as O*NET, is a database containing information gathered through job analysis. Information and analysis of over one thousand different jobs exist on this network. These are organized by the standard occupational classification system, which sorts specific requirements of any given job. The requirements are:

- Experience.
- Worker requirements.
- Occupational.
- Worker characteristics.
- Occupation-specific requirements.
- Occupation characteristics.

Rather than conducting extensive job analysis, many companies will find the job, or a similar job, on O*NET and use the descriptions from this database. This approach can be useful for companies who do not have the resources to perform detailed job analyses.

Job Descriptions

A job description outlines all the duties, responsibilities and individual tasks necessary for adequate performance of a job. Job elements are presented to indicate their importance in job performance. Job descriptions also include examples of specific tasks.

A job specification provides information about specific characteristics, skills and knowledge required of an individual to perform a job. These specifications can specify a certain amount of past experience in a similar job, a degree, or experience with certain types of software, equipment, or procedures.

The job description and job specification work together to show what a job entails and what kind of person would be most likely to be able to perform that job efficiently. A human resources manager can use this information during the recruiting and selection process to ensure employees are found who match the job requirements.

Legal Issues Involved in Job Analysis

Because job analysis is such an important part of the employee selection process, job analysis must be performed according to federal guidelines to ensure equal opportunity for all qualified applicants. In particular, the Americans with Disabilities Act (ADA) requires that job analyses outline essential job functions so that a company can make reasonable accommodation for disabled employees. Gender discrimination is also a concern raised in the course of a job analysis. Jobs previously performed by men are often seen as more complex or demanding than jobs previously held by women, possibly leading to discrimination in the hiring process.

Staffing

Recruiting

Internal Recruiting

Internal recruiting refers to the process of recruiting candidates who already work for the company to fill open positions. Internal recruiting usually leads to a promotion for an existing employee. This allows lower-level positions to be filled through external recruiting, usually resulting in lower recruiting costs for the company.

Advantages to internal recruiting include increased motivation for employees. Employees are motivated to work toward promotions and long-term career development. Internal recruiting also helps keep the corporate culture stable and maintains existing knowledge.

Disadvantages of internal recruiting include the possibility of stagnation within the company, because new ideas are not fostered. A ripple effect can also occur as employees are promoted and empty positions are left below them to be filled.

The two major methods of internal recruiting are job posting and supervisory recommendations. In job posting, information about the vacant position is disseminated throughout the company through internal communication such as memos, newsletters, or the intranet. In many companies, job openings must be posted internally before external recruiting begins.

Supervisory recommendations occur when the person in charge of filling a position requests information from supervisors about what existing personnel might be a good fit for the position. One legal ramification of supervisory recommendations is that supervisors must be careful to provide equal opportunity for all qualified candidates regardless of race or gender.

External Recruiting

When a company uses external recruiting, they look for prospective employees who are not currently employed by the company. It is usually used in conjunction with internal recruiting to provide a good balance of personnel, to maintain the corporate culture, and to continue to provide advancement opportunities within the company.

Advantages of external recruiting include the introduction of new ideas to the company and preventing long-term stagnation. It also helps reduce the ripple effect, caused when internal candidates are promoted through the ranks, leaving open positions behind them.

Disadvantages of external recruiting include a possible blow to employee motivation. If employees see too many external candidates filling higher-level positions, they might feel that opportunities for advancement and career development are more limited. External recruiting is also more expensive than internal recruiting.

Most companies make use of four major methods for external recruiting:

- Word-of-mouth. The company asks for referrals from existing employees. This method is inexpensive, but the pool of possible recruits is limited.
- Advertising. The company purchases advertising in local newspapers or other outlets. This method allows the company to reach a wide variety of people and can also help reduce the possibility of discrimination.

- Employment agencies. These include the state employment agency, private employment agencies, and executive search firms (also known as headhunters). This type of recruiting can be costly, especially when working with private agencies.
- College campus recruiting. This includes working with college placement offices as well as holding regular campus job fairs. College recruiting can bring a variety of new talent and ideas to a company.

ELECTRONIC RECRUITING

In many companies, electronic recruiting has become the major form of recruitment, and is used for both internal and external recruiting. Companies can publicize job openings via their websites, their company intranet, or through dedicated job search sites such as Monster.com. For very little cost, a company can publicize a job nationally or even internationally, ensuring exposure to a wide variety of candidates. Advantages of electronic recruiting include a low recruiting cost and the ability to reach a wide and diverse employment pool. Disadvantages include a tendency for many unqualified candidates to apply, leading to additional difficulties in the selection process. In some cases, electronic recruiting does not reach minority groups, since some minorities have limited computer access.

INTERNSHIPS

An internship combines methods of external and internal recruiting. Interns are typically found through external recruiting, but they remain temporary employees. If the intern then goes on to become a full-time employee, this can be seen as a form of internal recruiting. Although interns often are not paid a salary, the internship provides them with real-world experience in their chosen field. It also provides the company with a good idea of their work ethic, how they fit in the corporate culture, and how well they might perform a specific job in the long-term. Using internships to find appropriate long-term employment is becoming more and more popular, and has even extended into the electronic recruiting arena with the advent of electronic internships.

JOB PREVIEW

A job preview is any information provided to a prospective employee about how the job will be performed and how the employee will fit into the position. It is very important that the human resource manager ensure that these job previews are realistic. If the job is presented in terms that are overly positive, the applicant will be disappointed in the day-to-day reality of his position.

One way to present a realistic job preview is to allow a potential employee to observe an existing employee performing the job in question. Recruiters can also provide detailed descriptions of the day-to-day requirements and activities of a job. Realistic job previews have been shown to increase employee retention and job satisfaction.

SELECTION PROCESS

After recruitment has provided a group of candidates for a specific position, the selection process begins. The selection process consists of three main steps:

1. Information gathering. Specific information about the candidates is collected and organized. This can include experience, skills, education and other information supplied during the recruiting process.

2. Evaluation. In this step, the candidates are evaluated to eliminate those who do not meet the basic job requirements. For example, if the job requires a Master's degree, applicants who do not meet that requirement are eliminated.
3. Selection. Applicants are narrowed down to those that best meet the requirements of the job, and a final selection is made to fill the position or positions.

Selection Criteria

Selection criteria are criteria used to determine which applicant or applicants are best suited for a particular position. Some criteria are objective while others are not. Criteria typically include:

- Education—knowledge necessary to perform the job.
- Experience—past experience in performing the same or similar job duties.
- Skills and abilities—objective skills such as typing speed or ability to use specific software, and more subjective abilities like effective social interaction.
- Personal traits—personality characteristics that enable a candidate to interact well with the rest of the team.
- Proper "fit"—a combination of ability, personality and how well an individual reflects the corporate culture.

Employment Application and Background Checks

Employment applications are almost always the first step toward gaining employment with a particular company. Applications collect basic personal information about a candidate as well as information about their background, education and experience. Questions on an employment application should help determine if an applicant is qualified for and capable of performing a specific job. Some personal data, such as gender and age, may not be included on an application to prevent discrimination on the part of the employer.

Background checks are often used to verify that the information an applicant provided is accurate. For example, a prospective employer might confirm that an applicant holds a particular degree. In some cases, legal background checks are also performed to ensure an applicant does not have a criminal record.

Employment Tests

Employment tests are used to assess an individual's abilities, personality and overall intelligence, as well as other characteristics important to the job. Interviews are a form of employment test, since they are used to assess the individual on a personal level. Other forms of employment tests are actual paper and pencil tests, or tests performed in the form of a simulation of work to be performed in the course of the actual job. The types of employment tests used are determined by the requirements of the job, as well as by the managers and the human resources department.

Cognitive Ability Tests

Cognitive ability tests measure the applicant's intelligence in general or specific mental abilities such as reading comprehension or mathematic ability.

Psychomotor Ability Tests

Psychomotor ability tests measure physical skills such as hand-eye coordination, physical strength, dexterity or other physical abilities important to a job.

Personality Tests

Personality tests measure specific personality traits in an individual. These traits can indicate an individual's ability to do a job—for example someone who tests as an introvert might not do well in a position that requires extensive interaction with customers.

Integrity Tests

Integrity tests are designed to test an applicant's honesty and moral makeup. Although these tests are growing in popularity, many job applicants find them invasive and inappropriate.

Work Simulations

In a work simulation, the applicant is asked to perform a series of tasks that are related to the job for which they have applied. For example, an applicant who is expected to be able to use spreadsheet software might be asked to perform typical spreadsheet tasks on a computer. Typing tests are often used to assess an applicant's typing speed, and data entry tests can demonstrate an applicant's ability to perform every-day tasks that will be required in a data entry position. Applicants who will be required to operate specific machinery or drive a vehicle are often tested under supervision.

Interviews

The personal interview is among the most common types of selection techniques. In an interview, the applicant will talk directly to a manager, human resources personnel, or another representative chosen to evaluate his suitability for the job. There are four basic types of interviews.

Structured Interviews

The interview consists of pre-determined questions, all of which are presented to all the candidates. These questions are designed to relate directly to job requirements and provide consistency in the interview process.

Unstructured Interviews

These interviews are not planned in advance and tend to be extemporaneous, though questions are kept relevant.

Semistructured Interviews

These combine elements of structured and unstructured interviews.

Situational interviews

Questions are presented that describe a situation, and the applicant answers by discussing how he would respond to the situation.

Interview Errors

Errors can occur during the interview process that can affect the ability of the interviewer to make an objective selection decision. These errors include:

- Errors. An interviewer judges a candidate based on the previous candidate. If the previous candidate is particularly qualified, the next candidate, while equally qualified, might not seem like a good fit to an interviewer who was impressed with the previous candidate.
- Similarity errors. The interviewer assigns positive characteristics to candidates who resemble himself.

- First impression errors. The interviewer makes a judgment in the first few minutes of the interview. Events in the rest of the interview, even if they contradict this judgment, are not weighted as highly.
- Irrelevance errors. The interviewer is influenced by factors that have nothing to do with the candidate's qualifications.

References, Recommendations, and Assessment Centers

References and Recommendations

The candidate provides a recommendation letter from a previous employer or other business associate, or provides a list of individuals who can provide information about his past performance or other important characteristics. Some companies will only provide objective information about previous employees due to liability issues.

Assessment Centers

Used to select management employees, an assessment center is an event which assembles candidates in a single location where they are evaluated by existing managers. Candidates typically undergo testing and assessments of various types to determine their suitability for the job. Assessment centers can last two or three days.

Selection Decision

The final decision as to which candidate will be offered a job is based on how the candidates perform on the various selection techniques. Most companies use a combination of techniques to reduce the possibility that the chosen technique might skew the results. Depending on the job, the selection criteria might be objective—for example the chosen candidate might be the one who performs best on specific tests. Other companies and other positions might require a more subjective decision, such as choosing a candidate with the best personality fit. The final choice can be influenced by selection errors, resulting in a choice that does not work out well in the long run.

Legal Issues

Legal issues regarding employee selection are often tied to anti-discrimination policies. If a candidate can prove that he or she was overlooked due to race, gender or disability in spite of proven ability to do the job, the company could find itself involved in a lawsuit.

The human resources department should evaluate the company's selection system on a regular basis to ensure there is no discrimination involved. This evaluation also ensures that the selection processes used are the most efficient methods and provide the most accurate results. Utility analysis is an approach that evaluates individual selection techniques to ensure they provide the best possible results.

Reducing Number of Employees

There are several situations in which a company might find a reduction in force to be necessary. Three major reasons are:

- Work force numbers remain unsustainable in spite of normal attrition and retirement. If a company is in a slow growth or stable phase, or in a period of gradual downward growth, routine employee turnover might not be sufficient to reduce the size of the work force in relation to available finances.
- Economic forces lead the company to downsize. In the case of a recession or a rapid decline in demand for a company's products or services, the company may no longer be able to support its existing workforce.

- A merger between two companies results in duplication of job positions. In many cases when two companies merge, a workforce reduction results to eliminate jobs that are identical or even similar between the two companies.

Distributive, Procedural and Interactional Justice

How employees react to downsizing is largely determined by their perception of how they were treated by the company. The possible perceptions can be described by distributive, procedural and interactional justice.

- Distributive justice. An individual feels justly treated when he perceives that he has been dealt with similarly to others.
- Procedural justice. An individual feels justly treated if he feels that the procedures used to make a decision were fair.
- Interactional justice. An individual feels justly treated when he is treated with courtesy and respect during the decision-making process.

Layoff Strategy

An employee who feels he has been treated fairly is less likely to be angry or bitter about a reduction in force decision. A human resource manager should bear this in mind when managing a reduction in force operation. Based on the ideas of perceptions of justice, employees will respond better to a layoff when:

- The layoff appears to affect everyone equally, without specific people or types of people being targeted.
- The decision regarding whom to lay off was made fairly and the criteria for the layoff was explained clearly by management.
- The managers, human resources department, and others involved in bringing the news of the layoff did so respectfully.

Considering these issues and perceptions, when constructing a layoff strategy, can help the process go more smoothly and leave the employees who are laid off feeling as if the process was fair.

Downsizing Legal Issues

Downsizing can result in legal issues for a company if employees are not chosen objectively and specific legal guidelines are not followed. Some situations that can result in legal problems include:

- Disparate impact. Minorities and other protected groups such as older workers are affected more severely by the downsizing than other groups.
- Performance-based selection. Basing layoffs on employee performance can result in problems if job performance criteria are not clearly defined or if performance rating systems are not individualized enough to differentiate between specific positions.
- The WARN Act. This act requires companies to give employees sufficient time to make plans for their future employment in the case of a large layoff or facility closure. Failure to meet these guidelines can result in fines, penalties, and future legal action.

Termination of an Employee

In general, employees are terminated because they fail to perform to required standards. In most cases, the company will provide guidelines for the employee to improve his performance or will take disciplinary action before resorting to termination. In cases where an employee is ill or suffering from a specific condition that inhibits job performance, the company should provide help in the form of counseling or another form of employee assistance program (EAP).

The causes of sub-par performance include:

- The employee does not have the ability to perform the job.
- The employee was not trained properly.
- The employee has a specific physical or psychological problem making it difficult or impossible to perform his job.
- The employee lacks motivation to perform his job to appropriate standards.

Discipline

Progressive Discipline

Progressive discipline is a set of guidelines outlining how poor performance is dealt with. It consists of a progression of disciplinary actions that must be taken. If the employee does not improve performance during the course of progressive discipline, termination may result.

A typical progressive discipline plan might include:

- Verbal warning.
- Written warning.
- Suspension.
- Termination.

This procedure provides the employee with the opportunity to improve his performance or correct his behavior. It also provides the company with evidence that they gave ample opportunity and guidance to the employee before resorting to termination.

Positive Discipline

Positive discipline is similar to progressive discipline in that it presents a series of steps that must be taken to inform an employee of measures that must be taken to improve performance, as well as a series of warnings and occurrences that will end in termination. However, positive discipline is integrated with performance management in that the emphasis of the process is upon helping the employee correct behavior or improve performance. Positive discipline supplies support, counseling, and problem solving procedures to give the employee a clear idea of what must be done to improve performance or behavior. With a positive discipline approach, the employee often feels less threatened and more empowered, since the employee is closely involved with the process and is treated in a positive manner rather than a negative manner.

Employment-at-Will

In modern practice, terminating an employee can be a complicated process. Many company policies regarding termination are in place to prevent litigation regarding these decisions. However, legally, an employer can terminate an employee without providing a reason, and at any time. This is referred to as "employment-at-will."

Exceptions to employment-at-will occur when termination occurs due to discrimination or other factors, in which case the employee can sue for wrongful termination. Situations that can lead to a judgment of wrongful termination include:

- The reason for termination is in violation of a specific law such as the Civil Rights Act.
- Termination occurs in violation of a contract between the company and the employee.
- Termination occurs because the employee has alerted authorities to violations committed by the company (whistle-blower).

These exceptions can vary depending upon the state where the termination took place.

Wrongful Termination Lawsuits

Wrongful termination lawsuits can be expensive and embarrassing to a company. For this reason, many companies have procedures in place to decrease the possibility that an employee termination could lead to this kind of suit. These procedures can include:

- Procedures for progressive disciplinary action, giving an employee ample time and guidance in correcting his behavior and improving his job performance.
- Documentation procedures to ensure all the reasons for termination are properly recorded.
- Providing realistic performance evaluations as evidence that an employee has not performed up to requirements.
- Providing counseling or remedial training for employees with specific problems or for employees who have not been properly trained.

Following these basic guidelines can greatly reduce the potential for wrongful termination suits.

Voluntary Turnover

Voluntary turnover occurs when employees leave the company under their own volition. There are many reasons why an individual might leave a company, but the most common reason is dissatisfaction with the job.

Voluntary turnover is a natural part of business, and its effects on a company can be both positive and negative. Some side effects of voluntary turnover include:

- Costs to the company to replace an employee.
- When employees leave, opportunities for promotion are available for other people.
- Bringing new employees into the company also brings new ideas.
- Losing highly qualified, experienced employees can have a detrimental effect on the company.

There are five main steps to the basic model of the voluntary turnover process.

1. Dissatisfaction.
2. Employee considers leaving.
3. Employee looks for alternatives.
4. Employee decides to quit.
5. Employee actually leaves the company.

The places where an HR department is most likely to prevent turnover are step 1 and step 4. If the HR department can prevent the causes of job satisfaction, the employee will not become dissatisfied. In step 4, when the employee makes the decision to quit, HR can provide alternatives that will make staying in the existing job more attractive, such as increasing salary, improving conditions, or offering a transfer.

Employee Retention

In addition to making decisions about terminating employees, human resource managers must also focus on providing incentive for high performing employees to stay with the company. In some cases, employees leave for reasons over which the HR department has no control. In cases where employees depart or consider departure due to dissatisfaction with their jobs, HR can at times step in to keep the employee on the payroll.

For example, if an employee wishes to leave for a job with higher pay, HR can try to raise the employee's salary. If working conditions are not acceptable to the employee, HR can investigate and find ways to improve the situation. If an employee must relocate, HR might be able to approve a transfer if the company has a branch in the area, or arrange for a telecommuting job in order to maintain access to the employee's experience and talent.

Retention Strategies

Retention strategies exist to help keep employees working for the company. They are usually aimed at increasing job satisfaction. There are several types of retention strategies, among which are:

- Realistic job previews. If employees are given a detailed, realistic idea of what their job will be like before they begin working, they are more likely to be satisfied in their work.
- Job enrichment. Employees are given work they find to be more meaningful or more challenging or both, and employees are given more control over their work environment.
- Stock options. Employees can buy stock in the company, often at a reduced price. Typically, an employee must stay with the company a certain amount of time before they can benefit from stock options.

Job Embeddedness

Job embeddedness explains why some people remain at a job even though they are experiencing job dissatisfaction. Sometimes even extreme job dissatisfaction cannot overcome the idea of job embeddedness.

Job embeddedness occurs when factors outside the job itself outweigh the desire to leave the job. For example, the need to bring in a regular salary, ties to the surrounding community, a sense of loyalty to specific individuals at the company, or the need to maintain benefits for the employee or for the employee's family can keep an employee at a job even though he is not at all happy with his current situation.

Job Dissatisfaction

Job dissatisfaction can stem from a variety of causes. The most common are:

- The employee's natural inclinations. Some people are simply never satisfied with their situation.
- The kind of work being done. An employee might feel their work is too demanding or not demanding enough, or that their work is pointless in the context of the company.
- Wages and benefits. An employee might feel that his salary is too low, or that benefits are not sufficient for his needs. Dissatisfaction can also occur if an employee feels his wages or benefits are not commensurate with those offered to other company employees.

- Dislike of supervisor or fellow employees. Personality conflicts between employees and their supervisors, and between employees and their coworkers, are a common cause of job dissatisfaction.

Though the major long-term effect of job dissatisfaction is voluntary turnover, it can also have other effects that are detrimental to the employee as well as the company.

These include:

- Employees are absent or late more often.
- Lack of commitment to the job or the company itself (organizational commitment).
- Reduction in activity that helps the company but is not a defined requirement of the job (organizational citizenship behaviors, OCBs).
- Increased stress.
- Job burnout.
- Increased illness.
- Decreased productivity.

All of these side effects can spread to other employees, causing them to also become dissatisfied. They also can be costly to the company as performance declines and employees are paid for days when they are not actually working.

Employee Transfer

Employee transfers occur when an employee moves from one company location or subsidiary to another. Transfers can occur at the request of the company or at the request of the employee. Some common reasons for transfers include:

- The employee receives a promotion that requires a transfer.
- The location requires an employee with specific skills or needs additional staff.
- An employee's spouse is relocating to another area.
- An employee is not satisfied with his current location.
- An employee wishes to relocate to care for a family member or to be closer to family members for specific reasons.

Companies must have a defined process for requesting transfers. The human resources department must also have a defined process for deciding whether or not to grant a requested transfer. As with terminations and other employment issues, these procedures must prevent discrimination.

Monitoring Employee Job Satisfaction

In order to keep employees from leaving due to job dissatisfaction, many companies monitor overall satisfaction in the workforce. Job satisfaction is usually measured using a survey. Some companies make their own surveys while others use pre-designed surveys.

One common type of survey is a job descriptive index (JDI). The JDI divides the job into various elements including compensation, the type and amount of work done, and satisfaction with supervisors and how supervision is handled. Employees rank each element according to adjectives supplied on the survey. From these rankings, employers can assess overall job satisfaction.

One drawback to these surveys is that they can skew results over time. Overall employee satisfaction might seem to have increased when, in reality, those employees who were the most dissatisfied have simply left the company.

Training and Development

Training and Development

Training and development are two parts of a whole, but are somewhat different from each other. Training usually refers to teaching employees specific job skills, knowledge they must possess to do their jobs, and how they must behave for successful job performance. Training by definition is usually focused more on employees performing technical duties or involved in company operations.

Development, on the other hand, usually refers to management level employees and focuses on less specific skills such as employee management, company policy, time management, motivation, and problem solving. Rather than teaching an employee how to do a specific job, it helps them learn skills that will help in their current job as well as help them move into higher-level positions.

Orientation

Orientation is the process of introducing a new employee to the company's policies and procedures, the day-to-day requirements of his job, company culture, other employees, and any other details the employee might need to know in order to function efficiently in his new position. Without orientation, new employees can feel adrift, unable to do their jobs, and can even find themselves experiencing negative performance reviews for the simple reason that they do not know what they are required to do in the course of their jobs. Since the orientation process often involves a formal or informal introduction to company cultures, as well as a chance for the new employee to get to know the people he will be working with, orientation also helps employees feel more a part of the company.

Most companies have a procedure in place to help new employees acclimate to their new positions. Some approaches to job orientation include:

- Formal, classroom-style training.
- On-the-job training.
- Coaching.
- Guidance from a supervisor or another employee.

Depending upon company policies and the type of job being performed, new employee job orientation could consist of any combination of these approaches. Since different people learn in different ways, one or more of these approaches might be more effective for some employees than for others. Overall, the more comfortable a new employee feels with his job duties, the more likely he is to be satisfied with his job in the long term.

Another important part of orientation is orientation to corporate culture. The way a company functions on a social level often determines many subtle elements of how jobs are performed, how new employees are accepted into the organization, and how employees and supervisors interact. An employee coming from a company with a very informal corporate culture, for example, might find himself feeling out of place in a more formal company if he is not provided with an orientation that will clarify these aspects of corporate culture. Corporate culture orientation can be formal, held in a classroom setting, or can be presented during the course of a workday. Many aspects of corporate culture are difficult to quantify, and therefore must be absorbed over time.

Career

A person's career is a concept that encompasses an individual's entire body of work experience. A career usually consists of a progression of jobs, experiences, and other elements such as training, workshops, volunteer efforts and other activities that fit into the overall view of that person's work history. In most cases, a career focuses on progression through a single industry or type of work, but not necessarily a single company. For example, a person might pursue a career in construction, but work for a variety of companies in a variety of positions, eventually rising to management level. In the past, a person's career was more often seen as occurring within the context of a single company, but this idea has evolved with changing business practices and economic pressures.

A traditional career consists of four major stages:

- Exploration. An individual explores different options and opportunities, seeking work that most interests him.
- Establishment. An individual builds a place in his or her chosen field, learning the basics, progressing to more advanced positions and becoming knowledgeable and efficient.
- Maintenance. An individual reaches the highest point of their career, usually at a management level. From this position, many individuals choose to mentor others who are coming up in the ranks.
- Disengagement. An individual finds different priorities or interests, or feels she might be better fulfilled with other pursuits. She might reduce her responsibilities, leave the position for another type of work, or retire.

At one time, an individual was expected to pursue a career that would last his entire working life. Many people worked for a single company, and the disengagement stage ended with retirement.

Today, it is far more common for a person to undergo a number of exploration, establishment and mastery phases, often going through the entire cycle in a few years. Many people change careers based on personal preference, family needs, or simply a desire to change. Others find themselves changing careers by necessity as existing jobs change radically or disappear. In addition, more people find it easier to pursue advancement by moving to a new company rather than by moving up in rank in a single organization. Retirement has also changed, often leading to still another new career rather than an end to the formal work life.

Career Planning

Career planning occurs when an organization, in conjunction with an employee, provides and pursues job duties with an eye toward where the job will lead in the future. An employee might take on additional duties not normally associated with a job in order to learn skills that will enable a promotion. More commonly, the organization will provide professional development training that helps the employee develop skills that will help him secure promotions and move forward in his career.

Career planning helps the employee by giving him the opportunity to learn and practice new skills and to have the opportunity to advance in the company. It helps the organization by ensuring that employees are well-trained in advance of promotions, and by increasing job satisfaction so that employees are less likely to leave.

A number of benefits for the company are associated with career planning. Among these are:

- Lower costs.
- Higher motivation.

- Less absenteeism.
- Lower turnover.

Employees also experience benefits, including:

- Higher job satisfaction.
- Opportunities for education and career advancement.
- A clearer understanding of their place in the organization.

Career planning is limited in some ways, however. In some cases, an employee might not prove as well-suited for a promotion or a job change as expected. Changes in the company's needs could also shift an individual career path, or a more qualified candidate could usurp what an employee sees as his intended position. Also, a company might provide training, then an employee might choose to pursue an opportunity with another company.

Assessment Phase, Career Paths, and Career Counseling

In the individual assessment phase of career planning, an employee assesses his or her own skills and abilities, as well as goals. Many companies provide questionnaires to assist in this process.

Career paths are provided by the human resources department and represent a typical progression for an individual employee. In most companies, certain job positions are more likely to be connected to other, higher-level opportunities, creating a career path.

Career counseling involves discussion between employees and management regarding the most likely career paths for the employee, as well as the employee's skills and competencies. In this way, management personnel can be sure their ideas about an employee's progression in the company is in line with what the employee expects.

Employee "Buy-in"

Employee "buy-in" means that the employees undergoing training understand the motives behind the training and the long-term benefits it will have on their career as a whole. Feeling that the training is important and will help them improve their job performance, possibly leading to a raise or a promotion, provides strong motivation for individual employees. Training is much more effective if trainees are motivated. They are more likely to focus their attention on the task at hand and also more likely to retain information learned in the course of the training.

Effective Training Program

Employee training has six major purposes:

1. Improvement of knowledge and skills.
2. Teaching new methodology.
3. Teaching new techniques.
4. Teaching safety, particularly as regards equipment and machines.
5. Increasing morale.
6. Employee self-actualization.

The type of training used should match the types of skills or knowledge being taught. For example, if improvement of knowledge is the main goal of a training session, a straightforward classroom approach might be most effective. To teach new techniques or methodology, on-the-job training or training in an environment very similar to job conditions will be more likely to produce the desired results.

Training and Different Learning Styles

In education, teachers are expected to provide learning materials that work for students who learn in different ways. These same principles must be used in on-the-job training to ensure the best results for all those involved in the training.

The basic types of learning styles are:

- Visual.
- Auditory.
- Kinesthetic.

Too often in corporate training, only one style, usually visual or auditory, is used in any single training program. By providing materials that appeal to all styles of learning, training is much more likely to be successful and engaging for those involved. When those being trained are engaged, they will also have higher motivation and better long-term retention of the concepts being presented.

Modeling

A modeling approach is most often used to train specific procedures or techniques of performing a job. Someone who is experienced with the technique demonstrates it, usually with a narrative explaining what he is doing, and those learning the technique observe and listen. For the greatest effectiveness, the trainees then also perform the activity, usually with guidance from the trainer.

Modeling provides numerous advantages over other forms of training because the trainees can see the action being performed, hear a description of how it is performed, then actually perform the task. With visual, auditory and kinesthetic elements, modeling is a comprehensive teaching approach.

Real-Time Practice

Real-time practice provides trainees the opportunity to perform new tasks in a realistic setting. The setting might be a simulation of actual working conditions, or the training might be administered in an on-the-job setting. Either way, the task must be performed in "real-time," that is, exactly as it would be if performed during the course of the job.

Real-time practice provides many of the same advantages of modeling, in that the task is usually demonstrated and narrated by the trainer, and then reenacted by the trainee. This provides the opportunity for the trainee to absorb the information in a variety of ways, ensuring long-term retention and confidence in his ability to perform the task when required.

Coaching

Coaching as a teaching method is applicable both to employee training and employee development, as it can provide instruction in skills and tasks as well as more generalized guidance in managerial skills such as employee management and problem solving.

In coaching, an experienced employee will work with a trainee, usually in an on-the-job setting, side-by-side through the course of the workday. Combining modeling, real-time practice and even straightforward, classroom-like training as required, coaching lets the trainer respond to the trainee's learning needs continuously. The trainee is able to ask questions and receive immediate clarification of issues he does not understand. The coach can also provide immediate feedback, ensuring that the trainee can improve his performance as needed.

APPRENTICESHIP

The apprenticeship has been a staple in career development for hundreds of years. An inexperienced trainee is brought into a company or business and trained by experienced workers over a period of time. In the past, the apprenticeship was used largely by craft guilds to teach skilled labor, and apprentices were expected to remain with their masters for a period of time to provide labor in return for their training.

Apprenticeships are still used in various vocations. In others, a similar approach is used but it is referred to as an internship. An individual works with the company in a training capacity, usually without pay, and is often then offered a permanent position with the company. Apprenticeships or internships benefit both the employee and the company by providing extensive training for the employee and well-trained future employees for the company.

REFRESHER COURSES

Often, after a few years on the job, an employee might forget how to perform tasks he uses infrequently, or find that he has performed the same task so many times that the habits developed over time have reduced the quality of his performance. In these cases, refresher courses can help the employee get back on track.

Many professions that require complex technical skills or up-to-date knowledge of new techniques or legal regulations require refresher courses on a regular basis. This includes doctors, lawyers, and other professions. These refresher courses help ensure that individuals are able to perform their jobs as efficiently as possible and use the most advanced techniques available.

PROGRAMMED LEARNING

Programmed learning is basically training in a traditional classroom setting. This is one of the most common training approaches used in companies, though it is not always the best approach for all job skills. In general, the trainer teaches the material and the trainee is tested on it. Hands-on practice may or may not be included in the training sessions.

The advantages to programmed learning are that the method is relatively easy to prepare for and to present. Disadvantages are that it is not necessarily suitable to all topics, and does not supply material that appeals to all learning styles, meaning some trainees will respond better than others. Those who do not respond well to this teaching approach will most likely be less motivated and will not retain the information in the long term.

VESTIBULE LEARNING

In vestibule learning, training occurs off-site, but the training facility is structured to be similar to the actual work environment. Trainees can perform tasks and learn skills in a context that allows them to understand how the tasks and skills will relate to their job when they return to work.

Advantages to vestibule learning include the realistic nature of the training. Trainees do not have to figure out how the training applies to their jobs—it is immediately apparent due to the approach and setting. Disadvantages include the expense of renting or providing a training facility and of maintaining a training staff with sufficient experience to provide effective training.

ON-THE-JOB TRAINING

In on-the-job training, trainees are taught as they perform their job duties. All tasks and duties are performed "live," during a routine work day. Additional tasks might be addressed as needed, even if they are not everyday duties. The trainer in on-the-job training is usually someone who is familiar with or who is currently employed in the position the trainee is learning. In some cases, on-the-job training is performed by a new employee's predecessor before the previous employee departs the company or the position.

On-the-job training is highly effective because it presents all the duties and demands of the job in real time, as well as in the exact environment and conditions the employee will be performing in throughout his tenure on the job. Another advantage of on-the-job training is the opportunity for a trainee to learn from a highly experienced trainer.

Career Counseling

Career counseling is usually an ongoing program provided to a company's employees. It consists of various opportunities for employees to attend programs such as workshops, targeted counseling programs (specifically for women or minorities, for example), conferences or time spent at a career development center. These programs provide overall development and training as well as networking and the opportunity for employees, particularly managers, to feel more an integral part of the company.

Other career counseling can occur in less formal settings. This can involve discussions between an employee and his or her manager. Most commonly, career counseling occurs during performance appraisal, when a manager provides feedback on an employee's performance and discusses various aspects of the job and how the employee's career path might proceed.

Job Rotation

In job rotation, employees work in various positions throughout the company, learning about these positions and the various departments within the company. Experiencing the duties of a variety of different jobs helps the prospective manager understand how the company works and how the different departments cooperate and interact. For a manager who will be overseeing several departments, or will be ensuring efficient interaction between one department and others in the company, this type of development can be invaluable.

Planned Progression

In planned progression, an employee can experience increasing levels of responsibility and performance, as well as compensation, while remaining in the same position. This progression leads to promotions, as well, usually following a series of jobs up the ladder in an anticipated order. Many companies have a pre-determined path through which employees are expected to progress in order to move up in the company. These paths, along with training and development that occurs during the course of their time in each position, makes up the basis of planned progression as a form of employee development.

Temporary Promotions

Much like job rotation, a temporary promotion provides an employee with a look at other positions within the company as well as the responsibilities and duties they require. An employee with appropriate qualifications can spend a short amount of time at a higher-level position to get a better idea of what would be required of him at that position. Returning to his regular job, he will then know what path to take to prepare for an eventual move into that higher-level position. In most cases, the duration of the temporary promotion is determined ahead of time, and the employee is compensated at the higher level. After the pre-determined time has elapsed, the employee may return to his previous position or, in some cases, take on the higher-level position on a permanent basis.

Junior Board or Committee Method

In this approach to employee development, employees function as board members would function. They review specific issues within the company and come up with solutions. This approach is commonly used among non-profit companies, and is often focused on younger employees who want to learn more about the company and how it is run. It provides participants with the opportunity to see the "nuts and bolts" of a company's workings, and to get an idea of how they might approach specific problems and challenges within the company.

Performance Appraisals

Performance Appraisal

Performance appraisals are used to determine whether or not an existing employee is effectively performing his or her job. In most companies, each employee has a performance appraisal once or twice a year. The results of the appraisals are often used to determine if an employee should receive a raise or a promotion. In cases where the employee is not performing up to required standards, the performance appraisal might result in a plan to improve performance or, if the inadequate performance has gone on over a period of time, disciplinary action or termination.

Performance appraisals can increase employee motivation, since employees know that if they perform well they are likely to receive a positive appraisal and thus a raise or promotion. It also helps the company keep detailed records of employee performance in case a termination becomes necessary.

The major goal of the performance appraisal is to improve employee performance. The other goals of performance appraisal all contribute to this goal and include:

- Providing an objective measurement of employee performance and effectiveness.
- Providing data to the company that can be used to justify decisions regarding employees, including raises, promotions and terminations.
- Providing employees with information about their own performance so that they can take appropriate measures to improve and thus secure a raise or promotion or prevent termination or other disciplinary action.
- Preventing discrimination by providing objective feedback about performance, separated from irrelevant factors such as gender, race or age.

Organization

The organization must ensure that a performance appraisal process and procedure is in place. This procedure must be easily available to all managers, and it should include clear information about how appraisals and related information are used. In addition, the organization should supply clear standards for job performance. These standards should be easily available to managers and also to the employees, so that employees clearly understand the requirements of their specific jobs. The organization will also determine how often appraisals are performed and when, whether on an employee's anniversary or on a specific date company-wide.

Rater

In most cases, the person who performs the evaluation will be the employee's manager or supervisor. Ideally, the supervisor will have guidance regarding standards of performance as well as an idea of the context in which the employee works. This knowledge should work along with specific performance standards to allow the rater to provide relevant, helpful and objective feedback.

The rater must also collect and evaluate data about the ratee's performance in the period of time between performance appraisals and be able to recall and properly assess this information at the time of the appraisal. After the appraisal, the rater must then pass the appraisal information along to the ratee. If there are performance problems, the rater should provide suggestions for improvement or an overall performance improvement plan.

Ratee

The ratee must be able to also be objective about his or her performance. If he receives negative feedback during an appraisal, he must be able to accept this feedback, as well as suggestions made by the rater about how to improve performance. If a ratee is overly hostile or negative about an appraisal, the appraisal process becomes difficult and uncomfortable, and will not result in positive change.

In some cases, negative feedback might be unfair, biased, or based on a rater's personal prejudice. If the ratee feels this is the case in an individual performance appraisal, he can bring these concerns to the human resources department for evaluation.

Ranking Methods

Several ranking methods are commonly used in performance appraisals:

- Simple ranking. The manager lists all individuals in order from best to worst performance. Easy to implement but does not necessarily reflect actual difference in performance between ranked employees.
- Paired comparison. Each employee is compared individually to every other employee to generate a ranking. Similar to simple ranking, with the same advantages and disadvantages.
- Forced distribution. Requires a certain percentage of employees to be ranked into each category, creating a normal distribution similar to a bell curve. Can be useful to limit merit pay, but distribution may be unrealistic or unfair.

360-Degree Feedback

The 360-degree feedback technique is one in which a performance appraisal is based on information from co-workers all around the person being evaluated. This provides a variety of sources from which to make the appraisal. Because the different sources will all have different perspectives on the employee's performance, this approach enables the manager to compare and contrast different feedback, determining the strengths and weaknesses of individual sources and producing an equitable final assessment based on a combination of all the different pieces of feedback. Sources of assessment can include peers, supervisors, and subordinates.

The 360-degree feedback technique provides several advantages over other feedback methods, including:

- Specialized feedback from specific departments can give a clearer view of an employee's performance.
- Providing comprehensive information about a variety of performance areas.
- Helping employees see how other employees view them.

Although 360-degree feedback provides a great deal of information which a manager can use to produce a performance assessment, the method does have some disadvantages. These include:

- Ratee must catalog and evaluate all the acquired information.
- Differences in perceptions must be dealt with.
- Difficult for employees to respond to conflicting feedback.

In many companies, 360-degree feedback is used only for feedback. In companies where it is used to make decisions, often a coach is employed to help interpret data.

Performance Diary

A performance diary is an ongoing record of an employee's performance. Those responsible for assessing an employee—for example, the employee's manager—will make notes of specific incidents or behaviors that he feels will be useful in his periodic appraisal. An example could be an incident in which the employee performed particularly well, or the opposite. In all cases, a performance diary should include precise information such as the date, time, and the people involved in the incident.

The performance diary is helpful for assessment because the manager has a written record of performance and is no longer dependent on his memory to recall how an individual employee performed over the course of the year, or the period of time since the last performance assessment.

Behaviors vs. Outcomes Appraisals

Appraisals based on behaviors track an employee's performance by how he or she performs specific elements of the job. These appraisals assume that if specific elements of the job are performed correctly, then the employee is performing his job well. It focuses more on the job process and is considered in many cases to be an objective means of evaluation. Feedback can focus on how to improve specific performance.

Appraisals based on job outcomes are focused on the results the employee generates. For example, if a salesperson were being evaluated, an appraisal based on behaviors might focus on number of phone calls made. An appraisal based on results would focus on the actual number of sales. Feedback might be less specific, since it is more difficult to determine which behaviors might be affecting the final outcome of performance.

Rating vs. Ranking Methods

In ranking methods, each rank must have a single employee matched to that rank. This can provide an unrealistic evaluation, since more than one employee might be performing at the same level. If all the employees are performing well, ranking does not reflect this, instead forcing the manager to place some employees in higher rankings and others in lower rankings.

Rating methods provide more flexibility, allowing each employee to be evaluated on his or her individual merits. Rating scales do not require each employee to have a different rating, and so employees with similar performance are rated as such.

Graphic Rating Scale

A graphic rating scale is very popular and is used in a wide number of companies. In a graphic rating scale, a statement is made about the employee, then the person rating the employee must choose an applicable rating. For example, the statement might be, "Employee has acceptable typing skills," followed by a rating from 1 to 5 or 1 to 10, with the low numbers representing poor performance and the high numbers representing better performance.

Ideally, individual attributes should be determined by the demands of the employee's job so that the ratings are directly applicable to performance. Some companies also include a statement that rates overall performance as well as individual aspects of performance.

Critical Incident Method

In the critical incident method, rating is based on specific incidents in which the employee performed particularly well or particularly poorly. Raters can provide not only a summary of the incident, but also explanations that tell why the incident represented good or bad performance, producing detailed feedback for the employee. This method works well in conjunction with a performance diary, in which the manager can keep notes regarding these critical incidents and how he sees them in the context of the employee's overall duties.

BARS

The BARS (Behaviorally Anchored Rating Scale) appraisal system is a graphic rating scale that is combined with the idea of the critical incident method. The BARS defines specific situations the employee will encounter during the course of his job. The employee's performance during these situations is then rated according to a graphic rating scale. For example, if an employee's job requires him to interact well with customers on the phone, this specific behavior will be rated on the BARS.

Although the BARS can provide important and relevant information, it is usually difficult and complicated to develop, leading to high costs. In most cases, development is undertaken by managers who work together to determine the specific critical incidents and how they should be rated.

BOS

The BOS (Behavioral Observation Scale) is similar to the BARS in that it is based on specific incidents that, if they occur in the course of the job, indicate effective performance. The BOS lists a wider variety and longer list of behaviors than the BARS. In addition, a manager using the BOS is able to rate the number of times an employee performs these activities in order to generate an overall performance rating. With its added detail, the BOS provides an even more detailed performance appraisal. The level of detail, however, also leads to increased time and expense in developing the rating system.

MBO

MBO (Management-by-objectives) is a highly personalized system for performance assessment. A manager and an employee meet to develop individualized goals for the employee. Progress in achieving these goals is discussed throughout the year. At the end of the year, a formal assessment process determines the employee's level of success in meeting the goals. The highly individualized nature of the MBO provides highly relevant data about job performance and an objective means of measuring this performance.

Though MBO is an accurate and effective way to determine an employee's job performance in respect to specific goals, care must be taken to prevent pressure to achieve these goals from reducing effective employee performance in other areas.

Determining the Best Performance Appraisal Methods

Unlike other decisions in the course of doing business, determining the best performance appraisal method is not a clear-cut process. The appraisal method that works best may depend upon the type of company, the managerial approach, or even the individual job. In some cases, a company might use different appraisal methods for different types of work within the company.

Appraisal methods developed within the company, by current managers and employees, are likely to prove more effective because the employees being appraised will feel more invested in the process. In addition, if employees feel the way they are appraised is fair and gives an accurate picture of the work they do and how well they do it, they will also be more likely to respond well to the process.

Contextual Performance

Some things employees do during the course of their work day are not specifically required according to their job descriptions. However, these tasks or actions are beneficial to the company and increase the value of the job and the employee performing it. These types of tasks are referred to as contextual performance.

Because these tasks are not required or defined in the job descriptions, many argue that they should have no effect on performance appraisals. However, most managers will take these into account when evaluating an employee, whether consciously or unconsciously. Contextual performance can make an employee seem more dedicated to his job, or a better fit for the company's corporate culture, and therefore will have an impact on how he is seen by his manager.

Appraisal Problems

Projection

A manager will appraise an employee higher if that employee is similar to him in some way.Error. A manager compares employees to each other rather than comparing each individual to an objective performance standard.

Distributional Errors

A rater tends to rate the entire group on one end or the other of the rating scale.

Halo Errors and Horns Errors

In these cases, a rater gives an individual a higher or lower rating based on one characteristic. For example, if the employee is very good with customers, the manager will rate other tasks higher, as well. If, by contrast, the employee is not as personable, the manager will rate the employee down across the board.

Performance Appraisal Evaluation

The main purpose of performance appraisal is to improve performance. Therefore, if a company's performance appraisal process leads to better performance from employees, the process can be judged effective. If, however, the appraisal process leads to lower performance, resentment among employees, or higher stress levels, appraisals should be restructured so that their results are more in line with what is desired. The human resources manager can assist in this process both by helping to formulate or revise the assessment process, and by observing the long-term results of the process. In addition, the HR manager can ensure that the performance appraisal process is objective and free of bias or results that could result in legal problems.

Job Evaluation

Job evaluation helps a company determine the appropriate compensation for a specific job based on its overall value to the company. Once its value to the company has been determined, this information is used to assign a wage or salary to the position. Job evaluation is intended to ensure that individuals receive compensation commensurate to the contribution their jobs make to the company as a whole. The wage or salary assigned to a specific job function can differ from company to company—provided there are no regulations to determine the necessary compensation, as in government jobs—depending upon the company's overall financial status and the importance of the individual job to that company.

Job Evaluation Methods

Classification System

Jobs are grouped together according to their relative value to the company and the level of skill needed to perform them. Compensation is defined for each individual grouping or job grade. Government jobs are classified in this way.

Point System

To use this system, jobs are broken down into a set of factors and each factor is assigned a point value. The job is then evaluated based on the number of points assigned to it. In most cases, the point system uses a point manual that defines job levels by the number of points.

Factor Comparison Method

Jobs are evaluated based on specific factors determined by the individual organization. Compensation is determined based on these factors. This is one of the most detailed but also one of the most complex types of job evaluation.

Legal Issues

As with hiring and terminations, legal issues can affect the process and results of performance appraisals. When appraisals are used as the basis for decision-making, such as which employees to keep and which to let go, care must be taken to ensure that there is no disparate impact—that is, that the appraisals do not consistently rate certain groups, such as minorities or women, lower than others. Because of these issues, the more objective an appraisal is, and the more directly related to performance it is, the less likely it is for problems to arise.

In cases where appraisals are used only for feedback, and not for decision-making regarding termination or layoffs, these issues are much less likely to lead to legal problems for the company.

Compensation Issues

Compensating Employees

A number of factors must be considered when a company determines its compensation strategy, including:

- Corporate strategy and how it integrates with business and human resource strategies.
- How well the company can recruit and maintain employees.
- The company's financial standing.
- Whether or not a union is involved.

All of these elements can affect the company's ability to provide higher levels of compensation, but can also determine whether there are guidelines that must be followed, such as those determined by unions, with regards to what compensation must be provided for specific employees. Combined with job evaluation methods, these factors determine how employees will be compensated, both how much they will receive and whether they will be paid hourly or provided with a salary.

Wages and Salary

In most cases, the term "wages" refers to hourly rates paid to employees. For each hour on the job, the employee receives a pre-defined amount of money. Jobs paid hourly wages are usually operational and are lower in the company's overall job hierarchy.

Salary refers to a specific compensation amount that is determined on an annual basis. Sometimes salary is also calculated as a monthly sum. Compensation does not depend upon the time the employee spends at his job, but instead is based on the value of the position to the organization. Salaried positions are typically managerial or professional level.

Wage and Salary Administration

Once the company has determined how compensation is to be determined, the system of ensuring compensation is properly distributed goes into effect. The process of enacting this system is called wage and salary administration. Some elements of wage and salary administration include:

- Adjusting compensation to reflect promotions or raises
- Providing programs to facilitate promotions and job development
- Maintaining pay secrecy
- Managing pay compression when it occurs

Wage and salary administration is a major part of the function of the human resources department.

Seniority and the Maturity Curve

In some companies, compensation is determined by the amount of time an individual employee has worked for a company. Employees who have a longer history with the company are said to have seniority over newer employees. Especially in union-controlled industries, seniority determines an employee's compensation, with specific increases in salary implemented based on years worked. This approach is also sometimes referred to as a maturity curve. Often on the maturity curve, increases in pay are greater for newer employees, under the theory that newer employees must acquire more skills and knowledge in the first few years of their employment. One side effect of this compensation strategy is that it encourages employees to remain with the company in order to gain the benefits of seniority.

Pay-for-Knowledge and Skill-Based Pay

In a pay-for-knowledge approach, compensation is tied to knowledge rather than specific tasks. Employees receive compensation for learning additional skills that enhance their ability to do their current job or that help them learn the basics of other jobs they might move to or be promoted into. This compensation method is often found to be more applicable to salaried workers.

Skill-based pay is similar, but is more often used for employees who are paid hourly wages rather than salaries. Employees receive compensation for learning specific new skills applicable to their current job or to other jobs in the company. Learning additional skills can make the employee more marketable for job changes and also can provide flexible scheduling since employees are trained in numerous duties.

Above-Market, Market, and below-Market Compensation Strategies

In market-based compensation strategies, compensation is determined based upon what the current wages are in the overall market for similar jobs. As the names imply, above-market pays more than the average, market pays about the same, and below-market pays below the average. There are advantages and disadvantages to all three, as follows:

- Below-market: Cost savings for the company. Often results in lower job satisfaction, higher turnover, and lower-quality employees.
- Market: Cost savings for the company. Employees might be offered additional benefits to attract higher-quality candidates.
- Above-market: High cost for the company. Can attract higher-quality candidates. Difficult to scale salaries down once higher amounts have become expected.

Minimum Wage

Minimum wage is the lowest wage that can be legally paid to an employee. Although minimum wage is occasionally revised, some feel that it is still too high or too low depending upon the viewpoint.

Minimum wage is federally mandated, but some states have chosen their own rates which are higher than those required by the government. This is often related to the cost of living of the particular area.

Those who feel minimum wage is too high often cite the impact on individual companies who must pay more for entry-level or basic positions, often populated by employees without a great deal of experience or training. Those who believe it should be higher often feel that minimum wage does not reflect the actual cost of living.

Pay Secrecy

Pay secrecy refers to whether or not a company prevents individual employees from knowing what other employees make. In most companies, specific information about wages and salaries is limited to those with a need to know, such as managers and human resources personnel. These organizations feel that an individual's compensation is a private matter, and that revealing compensation to other employees might lead to job dissatisfaction or resentment.

In other companies, pay is not kept secret. Often, in these companies, pay is based on performance, and the overall belief is that if lower-paid employees see the possibilities of pay given higher-level performance, they will be motivated to improve their performance. This approach is often used among commissioned employees. It is also common in organizations that are publicly funded, so that budgets for these organizations remain transparent.

Pay Compression

Under ideal conditions, a job that requires greater experience or higher ability receives higher compensation than one that requires less experience. However, sometimes a job requiring less ability receives compensation similar to one with much higher requirements. This is referred to as pay compression.

Pay compression tends to occur as a side effect of rising cost of living and changing market conditions. An employee can be hired into a high-level position at or near the market rate. A few years later, an employee is hired into a lower level position, but the market rate has shifted so that his salary is almost the same as that of the

previously hired employee in the higher level position. In many cases, the existing budget makes it difficult to correct the situation. The effects of pay compression can be detrimental, leading to dissatisfaction and employee turnover.

Merit Pay

Merit pay is a form of performance-based reward wherein employees who make a significant contribution to the company are rewarded with additional compensation. Merit pay is often based on performance appraisals, but must be related to a well-defined system. This system is referred to as a merit pay plan. In order to motivate employees to perform in order to receive merit pay, the way merit is measured must be clear to everyone involved. Without clear, objective goals and rewards, merit pay can be perceived as unfair, leading to dissatisfaction among employees.

Individual Incentive Plan

In most cases, employee performance is rewarded on an annual basis when raises or promotions are issued after an annual performance review. In the case of individual incentive plans, though, rewards are provided more promptly when an individual demonstrates exemplary performance. Incentive plans are usually tied directly to the profitability of the company as a whole and whether the individual employee contributes to that profitability. For example, an incentive plan might provide a percentage of company profit to employees who have provided exceptional performance, with the exact percentage granted to each individual determined by the level of that performance. One common form of individual incentive plan is commission sales, and some organizations supply non-monetary rewards such as extended vacations or other perquisites. As with other compensation approaches, individual incentive plans must be well defined with objective goals and rewards.

Sales Commissions

A common form of individual incentive plan is sales commissions. In jobs that focus on direct sales to consumers, sales people receive a percentage of their sales totals as part of their compensation. In some cases, the commission is the only compensation the employee receives. Others provide a salary with commissions added on as incentive for high quality job performance. In all cases, this portion of the employee's salary is always uncertain and can fluctuate, sometimes due to circumstances beyond the employee's control, such as economic factors that reduce consumer activity. In other cases, a sales person's job performance might lead to increased sales but not represent the best presentation of the product or the best type of interaction with individual customers.

Gainsharing

In addition to individual incentive plans, some organizations offer team or group incentive plans. For example, an entire department or team might be offered a reward based on productivity, overall sales, or another criterion on which performance is based. In gainsharing, rewards are given based on improvements in group productivity. Profits or money saved as a result of productivity efforts is shared among the group according to a formula.

One type of gainsharing is called a Scanlon plan. In these cases, employee teams are asked to make suggestions that can result in cost reductions for the company. Rewards are distributed throughout the organization, with more of the funds going to the employees than is put back into the organization itself.

Purposes of Compensation

Compensation is provided to employees to reward the contribution they make to the company's overall goals and function. Without compensation, individuals would have no motivation to help a company achieve its goals. Compensation is also used to reward employees who provide particularly valuable contributions to the company. It can also help guide employee behavior and productivity, since employees can gauge what level of performance and what behaviors are most important to the company based on what behaviors are more richly rewarded by the company's compensation strategy. Compensation also helps employees feel that they are valued by the company and that their efforts and skill are being appropriately rewarded.

Internal and External Equity

Internal and external equity are ways in which employees make comparisons between their salaries and those of others. From these comparisons, employees will make judgments about their own level of compensation, deciding whether it is fair and, based on these observations, judge how the company values their work.

Internal equity is when employees compare their compensation to that of others in the same company. If an employee discovers that his level of compensation is lower than that of others with similar skills and ability, he is likely to become dissatisfied.

External equity is when employees compare compensation to that offered for similar jobs in other companies. Perceptions of inequity can lead to higher turnover.

If an employee feels his compensation is lower than that of others with similar jobs and responsibilities within his company, he might become resentful and dissatisfied. Asking for and receiving a raise in pay can correct this response, but it is not always a possible outcome. Attitudes toward those making more money might become confrontational. Employees who feel they are not being adequately compensated, while others are, will suffer from low morale and might not trust their supervisors or the company itself. If an employee feels that the inequity is a result of discrimination, he might sue the company, and if jobs performed by women or minorities are consistently lower paid in a company or organization, the company could face severe penalties.

Employees who perceive that other companies are paying better salaries for comparable jobs can also become dissatisfied. Even if the internal equity for a particular job is acceptable, resentment can develop against the company for not providing comparable compensation. A common result of external equity issues is a higher turnover within the company. In addition, the company might be unable to hire adequate replacements for the employees who choose to leave if the pay they offer is below the average market for that job type.

Pay Surveys

It is often in a company's best interests to determine the average salary offered to individuals in specific positions in various companies in the area. With this information, they can evaluate their own compensation strategies to ensure external equity. Providing an equitable salary can help maintain employee satisfaction and lower turnover in the company.

Pay surveys are used to gather this information. These surveys are often performed by organizations and then are made available to anyone with an interest in the information. Some large companies will perform these surveys on their own, while others will outsource the task to a company specializing in pay surveys. Outsourcing increases the likelihood that information gathered will be accurate and properly interpreted, since the firm involved will be experienced in administrating the surveys.

Negotiating Salaries Via the Internet

In many cases, information about compensation for specific jobs in various companies is easily available online. A prospective employee can research pay levels for a particular job, determine what the market rate is for that job, and use that information to negotiate a salary with a prospective employer. This readily available information is very useful to the employee attempting to receive the best possible compensation, but can be problematic for a company who is attempting to cut costs or which has been affected by pay compression. By changing many of the rules regarding pay secrecy that have prevailed in business settings, the Internet changes the balance of power between the company and its employees and prospective employees.

Benefits

In addition to the direct compensation provided by a wage or salary, many companies also offer additional types of compensation. These are collectively referred to as benefits. In some cases, a desirable benefits package can offset lower wages, attracting high-quality employees even if the salary offered is below market.

Common benefits include:

- Insurance
- Retirement programs
- Vacation
- Paid holidays
- Daycare

Some benefits are required by law, such as unemployment insurance, while others are provided based on the corporate compensation strategy.

Costs of Benefits

While it would seem logical to assume that the vast majority of costs to maintain an employee would go toward that employee's salary, this is not necessarily the case. On average in the US, about sixty percent of the cost of a single employee is accounted for by salary. The other forty percent is paid out in the form of benefits. Any company's compensation strategy must take these issues into account.

In other countries, the cost can be even higher. In the US, fewer benefits are legally mandated, and thus benefits cost less on average than in countries where there are far more mandated benefits.

Many European countries require far more mandated benefits than those required in the US, for example.

Why Companies Offer Benefits

A popularly cited theory regarding the value of benefits is the efficiency wage theory. This posits that employees who are provided with better salaries and better benefits will be happier and more productive, thus offsetting the cost of the benefits and salary by increasing company profits. In truth, most employees are less likely to leave a company if they are happy with the compensation they are receiving.

Sometimes companies will provide additional or different benefits to accommodate certain types of employees. For example, more companies have recently been offering daycare facilities for parents to make it easier for them to manage the demands of work and family. Health insurance programs are also often formulated to meet the needs of employees with families.

Mandated Benefits

Mandated benefits are required by law, or are regulated in some way by law. A company must supply these benefits to its employees, or must ensure that they are administered according to regulations. In general, mandated benefits are programs designed to assist employees when they lose income or their income is reduced due to specific circumstances such as illness, disability or retirement. They also assist an employee's family if the employee dies. Among these benefits are unemployment insurance, worker's compensation and social security.

Social security and unemployment insurance were both mandated by the same law—the Social Security Act of 1935. Social security itself refers to the Old Age Survivors and Disability Insurance Program, and is designed to provide supplemental income to retired individuals. Individuals pay into the social security program throughout their working life, and are entitled to partial benefits at sixty-two years of age. Full benefits are available after age sixty-seven.

Unemployment insurance functions as a stopgap income source for those who have lost their jobs. Specific requirements must be fulfilled in order to qualify for unemployment insurance, and it can only be collected for a certain amount of time.

Worker's compensation helps employees who have been injured while on the job, and helps replace lost income during recovery.

Nonmandated Benefits

Nonmandated or voluntary benefits are those offered by a company that are not required by law, though some nonmandated benefits are regulated by laws that provide guidelines or regulations regarding how they are administrated. Companies often offer benefits to make employment more attractive to high-quality candidates.

Common types of nonmandated benefits include:

- Insurance.
- Pension plans.
- Vacation and holidays.
- Miscellaneous benefits such as childcare.

These benefits are generally intended to help the employee on a day-to-day basis, to defray costs of common living expenses, and to reward the employees for their work.

Other Types of Nonmandated Benefits

Some companies pride themselves on their benefits packages, and provide special programs to their employees to make working for the company that much more attractive. Some of these benefits can include:

- Childcare. On-site childcare or day care has become more common as more companies work to cater to working mothers and families.
- Wellness programs. Maintaining employee health increases productivity and reduces health care costs.
- Care for elderly family members. Companies offer referrals to help those dealing with the challenges of caring for elderly parents or other family members.
- Miscellaneous perquisites. Companies might offer club memberships, free lunches, free coffee, stocks and bonds, a company vehicle, or on-site facilities for exercise or entertainment.

Insurance Coverage and a Private Pension Plan

Due to the cost of health care in the US, health insurance coverage has become a major and even essential part of any employee benefits option. Insurance premiums are split between the company and the employee, with the company taking a larger percentage. Some companies also provide vision, dental and prescription drug coverage, or offer membership in a health maintenance organization (HMO). Other types of insurance commonly offered include disability insurance and life insurance.

Private pension plans are funded by contributions made by the employee. These contributions are often matched by the company, doubling the fund's value. Pension plans are usually supplied in the form of an individual retirement account (IRA) or a 401(k).

Defined Benefit Plans and Defined Contribution Plans

In a defined benefit plan, the amount of compensation the employee receives is based on a predetermined formula. Benefits are not determined by the employee's contributions, but are usually based on the number of years of service.

A defined contribution plan means that the benefit provided to the employee is dependent on the contributions made by the employee and/or the employer. If only the employer contributes, this is known as a noncontributory plan. If both contribute, this is known as a contributory plan.

In all pension plans, the funds contributed into the plan are invested. How these funds are invested is regulated by law to prevent the loss of the funds in case of major economic downturns or issues with the company stock, which often represents a portion of the employee's investments.

Paid Time Off

Paid time off is a common benefit that allows employees to celebrate holidays, attend to personal errands or family issues or to take vacations. In most companies, paid time off includes:

- Paid holidays. Most companies provide about ten paid holidays per year, including Memorial Day, Labor Day, the 4th of July, Christmas, Thanksgiving and New Year's Day.
- Vacation time. The number of available days typically increases according to the amount of time the employee has worked with the company.
- Personal days. Additional days to be reserved for personal emergencies or other issues.

- Sick leave. If employees come to work while sick, they are not as productive and can spread illness to other employees, reducing productivity overall. Policies regarding sick days vary from strict, requiring a doctor to provide documentation, to more lenient.

Cafeteria-Style Plan

In cafeteria-style plans, the employee is presented with a list of benefits from which to choose, as well as a budget allotted by the company to pay for these benefits. The employee may choose the benefits from the list that he feels will be most beneficial to him. These plans can be difficult to administer, and sometimes do not result in an employee having the benefits package that will work best for his circumstances. In addition, since employees are likely to choose benefits they will use, the cost of more expensive benefits cannot be spread out over a wide number of employees. This is known as adverse selection, and also adds to the cost of this type of benefits structure.

Evaluating a Benefits Program

Companies must invest time and effort into evaluating their benefits programs, largely because these programs are a large expense. There are several ways for a company to assess the costs of its benefits programs, including:

- Wage surveys. The same forms used to assess compensation can also be used to assess benefits. In these cases, the company will receive information about how its benefits packages compare to those of other, similar companies.
- Internal auditing. The company can audit their costs to ensure benefits remain affordable to the company.
- Performance and recruitment auditing. If employee performance and satisfaction remain high, and recruitment continues to be successful, this might be an indication that the benefits package offered is attractive to current and prospective employees. In-house surveys can gather additional information about these issues.

Safety and Health

Safety and Health Hazards

Workplace safety hazards refer to work conditions that could cause an employee physical harm. This can refer to circumstances in which safety rules and guidelines are not followed, the presence of dangerous equipment, or inadequate maintenance on machinery or equipment.

Workplace health hazards produce a less immediate risk, but are potentially just as dangerous as safety hazards. Health hazards occur when a workplace environment contains elements that, over time, can adversely affect an employee's health. This could involve atmospheric problems such as poor ventilation, the presence of asbestos, or toxic chemicals to which employees are systematically exposed during the course of the job.

Occupational Illness

Occupational illnesses fall into seven major categories.

1. Lung disease caused by dusts of various kinds
2. Poisoning
3. Reoccurring trauma
4. Skin problems
5. Breathing problems caused by toxic compounds
6. Illness resulting from exposure to physical elements
7. Miscellaneous illnesses

Some occupations are more likely to present the danger of occupational illness than others. Companies that manufacture toxic substances are more likely to expose employees to toxic substances that can bring on occupational illness. Companies housed in unsafe buildings are more likely to present a risk of occupational illness.

Workplace Accidents

Common causes of workplace accidents fall into three major categories:

- Overall physical workplace environment. Accidents can occur due to elements of the environment such as wet floors, improperly shielded machinery, or even poorly installed carpeting.
- Defective equipment. If equipment and tools are not properly maintained and checked periodically for problems, injuries can occur.
- Employee actions. Employees might take actions that increase the hazards in the workplace. Not following safety guidelines, not using recommended equipment or using equipment improperly, or interacting improperly with other employees can increase the risk of injury on the job.

Preventing Workplace Accidents and Occupational Illness

Workplace accidents can be reduced or prevented by monitoring the conditions under which work is performed. Safety engineers can work with a company to evaluate the work environment as well as how work is done and how equipment is maintained. They can make recommendations to mitigate or eliminate dangerous situations before they lead to accidents. Protective gear and extensive employee training accompanied by a reward system for days without accidents can also greatly reduce the occurrence of workplace accidents.

Occupational disease can also be reduced if a company and its employees are aware of the risks involved in their jobs. The company should take precautionary measures or attempt to correct the hazardous nature of the environment, as well, to reduce the long-term effects of exposure to toxic elements.

ELEMENTS AFFECTING HEALTH AND SAFETY

Several aspects of the workplace must be considered when providing a safe, pleasant work environment, including:

- Sufficient light.
- Appropriate temperatures.
- Ergonomic office design.
- Work schedule.
- Overall workplace design.

These elements not only affect the employee's safety, health and comfort, but can also have a major effect on overall employee satisfaction. Employees who feel their work area is comfortable and well-lit, and who are not required to work excessive hours that lead to fatigue, are more likely to be satisfied with their jobs, as well as less likely to be involved in accidents. A workplace that is not structured to isolate individual employees also contributes to a better overall workplace atmosphere and a higher level of job satisfaction.

STRESS

Stress is all too common in today's workplace, and can be quite severe. Severe stress takes a toll on the immune system, leading to greater absenteeism as employees become ill more often. It can also lead to hypertension, substance abuse, insomnia, depression and other systemic health problems. Causes of workplace stress include:

- Lack of job security.
- Hostile work environment.
- Sexual harassment.
- Burnout.
- Work overload.

Other results of stress can include:

- Absenteeism.
- Job dissatisfaction.
- Inappropriate job behavior such as theft.
- Aggression or violence on the job.

The employer can assist in managing stress by ensuring that the workplace environment is not hostile and by preventing work overload. They can also supply stress-reducing programs such as exercise programs or fitness centers on-site.

WELLNESS PROGRAMS

Many companies have instituted wellness programs to help employees deal with stress, as well as to help maintain overall health and well-being in the workplace. These programs are usually institutional programs or collateral stress programs.

Institutional programs are policies that apply to the company as a whole, such as specific work schedules, a corporate culture that does not discourage vacation or other time off the job, and policies that help supervisors understand the long-term effects of work overload and burnout. These policies are intended to prevent excessive stress from occurring.

Collateral stress programs exist within the company to help with stress management. These can include fitness programs, assessment and screening programs to help detect stress, or compensation for anti-stress efforts taken off-site.

Job Security

Job security is the sense that your job is not in danger, and that you will continue to have a place to work and a source of income for the long term. Employees who are constantly worried about job loss, whether due to economic issues, supervisor attitudes, or personal anxiety, suffer from much higher levels of stress than those who are not. Perceived lack of job security can lead to poor performance, lowered productivity, aggression toward employees perceived to have more secure positions, increased illness and absenteeism, and other side effects related to long-term stress. Companies who believe employees can be spurred to better performance through threats of termination contribute to stress in their employees by undermining their sense of job security.

Business Security

In addition to providing a safe, healthy environment for employees, businesses also must take into account the security of their business operations, data, facilities and equipment. Companies who work with highly sensitive materials will put security measures into place to protect their business. In some cases, these measures can create an uncomfortable atmosphere in which employees can feel as if the company does not trust them.

Balancing business security with employee comfort and job satisfaction is a complex task. If employees are unable to access personal email or communicate with family members during the workday, this could create a difficult environment, especially for parents of small children. On the other hand, businesses with highly proprietary systems must take necessary measures to prevent infiltration or proliferation of viruses.

Employee Rights and Discipline

Homeland Security

After the tragedy of September 11, the US began to institute stricter guidelines for many issues regarding Homeland Security. Businesses also put strict guidelines into place regarding several issues that affected employment and business security. Many large companies also put into place emergency preparedness programs focused specifically on responding to a terrorist attack.

Some major ways in which Homeland Security can affect the human resources function include:

- Stricter regulations regarding hiring non-citizens.
- Increased difficulty obtaining work visas, even for highly qualified candidates.
- Less stress on international recruiting.
- Changes in regulations for travel, especially international travel.

Many of these measures, as well as the awareness of possible terrorist attacks, have also produced a long-term effect on the overall sense of security among the general American public.

Individual Privacy Versus Business and National Security

The argument about privacy versus security is a long-standing one, but the conflict has come to greater attention since 9-11. The Patriot Act, intended to reduce the likelihood of terrorist acts on America soil, has come under fire from some because of the perceived violation of the privacy of individuals. On one side of the argument, this increased scrutiny of individual citizens helps provide protection for the American people in general, allowing us to maintain our overall freedom as American citizens. On the other side, the added bureaucracy and invasion of privacy erodes the rights US citizens have come to expect from their government. In addition, many feel the safeguards could be too easily misused and too widely applied, infringing on individual rights more than ensuring protection and safety for all citizens.

Regulation

Enacting regulations that affect human resources management occurs in three basic phases:

- New regulations are created by national, state or local government.
- Regulations are enforced through a specific entity, such as a new agency, new regulatory commission, or an existing agency that is assigned the task of enforcing the regulations.
- Regulations are implemented and put into regular practice.

Depending upon the clarity of the regulation, it might be relatively simple to enforce and implement, or it might be open to various interpretations, leaving the human resources department to work out how best to comply with regulatory guidelines.

Equal Employment Opportunity (EEO)

EEO is designed to prevent the practice of illegal discrimination in the workplace. This means that hiring, promotion, wages, and other job-related decisions should be based on objective factors related to specific performance, time on the job, or other defined parameters. These decisions cannot be based upon race, gender, ethnicity or other personal factors.

The Civil Rights Act, passed in 1964, was enacted in order to manage these issues. In Title VII of this important act, it is stated that no employer who falls into categories defined by the act may fire or refuse to hire an individual based on defined personal factors including race, religious belief, nationality or gender. This act also established the Equal Employment Opportunity Commission (EEOC) as a regulatory body to ensure the law was properly followed.

Disparate Treatment, Disparate Impact, and the Four-Fifths Rule

Discrimination in the workplace can be defined in several ways according to the law. Some litmus tests for discrimination include:

- Disparate treatment. Persons with similar jobs and duties are treated differently, and this different treatment is directly related to their race, gender, national origin or other characteristic defined by EEO.
- Disparate impact. A specific business policy or practice excludes a higher proportion of a protected group than other members of the population. One way to determine disparate impact is by comparing the characteristics of a group of employees at a particular company to the characteristics of the available qualified candidates.
- Four-fifths rule. This is a means of determining disparate impact. If a specific requirement for employment results in a selection that represents less than 80 percent (four-fifths) of the employees selected from other groups, disparate impact is a factor.

Bona Fide Occupational Qualification (BFOQ)

In some cases, a business may feel that they have a specific need that requires the choice of one type of employee over another—that is, an individual of a certain protected or non-protected group will simply be more capable of performing the job. These exceptions to EEO are very rare, and the company must be able to prove that there is a business necessity related to their decision to hire a specific type of individual. The preference of the company's customers does not qualify as a factor—for example, if a business' customers would prefer to be waited on by men rather than women, the company may not cite this as a business necessity to justify a refusal to hire women.

Pattern or Practice Discrimination

Pattern or practice discrimination occurs when a specific group is systematically discriminated against. An example would be a company that, across the board, does not hire or promote African-Americans. In order to qualify as pattern or practice discrimination, the practice must affect more than just a single individual. An accusation of pattern or practice discrimination must prove that the discrimination is practiced on a wide scale and deliberately affects individuals of a protected class. If a sampling of qualified candidates from outside the company presents a widely different range of individuals in protected classes than a sampling of existing employees, pattern or practice discrimination might exist within that organization.

Protected Classes

Protected classes are groups of people with similar characteristics who are protected from discrimination by equal employment opportunity laws. EEO uses specific characteristics to define protected classes, including:

- Gender.
- Religion.
- Ethnicity.
- Country of origin.
- Skin color.
- Race.
- Age.

- Disability.
- Veteran status.

Though laws can vary as far as how and to what extent each protected class is protected, these groups constitute the major categories of protected classes. In addition, these regulations are not intended to favor protected classes at the expense of unprotected classes, but simply to provide fair treatment for all individuals.

Affirmative Action

Many companies have taken systematic action to ensure discrimination does not occur, or to correct the long-term effects of past discriminatory practices. This approach is referred to as affirmative action, and is intended to balance the proportion of protected classes working at the company.

Affirmative action plans typically involve three steps:

1. Utilization analysis. In this stage, the company compares the make-up of their workforce to that of the available qualified candidates to calculate the amount of disparity.
2. Timetables and goals. The company develops a plan describing the exact goals of the affirmative action plan and when these goals should be accomplished.
3. Action steps. The company determines what actions will effectively accomplish the goals set by the affirmative action plan.

Sexual Harassment

Not only does EEO seek to prevent discrimination, but it also works to guarantee a safe environment for protected classes. The most common form of harassment in the workplace is sexual harassment.

Sexual harassment usually falls under one of two categories:

1. Quid pro quo. An individual is promised a raise, promotion or other advantage in the workplace if he or she provides sexual favors to a supervisor.
2. Hostile work environment. This occurs when co-workers subject an individual employee to behavior that makes her uncomfortable. A hostile work environment can lead the harassed employee to suffer from extreme stress, reduced productivity and even physical and emotional harm.

Though sexual harassment is usually perpetrated by males toward females, it can also be directed by females toward males, or be perpetrated between members of the same sex.

Typical Disciplinary Problems

The major workplace disciplinary problems fall into five basic categories.

- Performance problems
  - Missing deadlines
  - Work errors
  - Quality issues
- Attendance problems
  - Arriving late
  - Leaving early

  - Not showing up for work at all
- Ethical issues
  - Accepting bribes, gifts or other inappropriate compensation
  - Filing false records
  - Claiming another's work
- Behavioral problems
  - Harassing other employees
  - Vandalizing or sabotaging equipment
  - Using controlled substances or alcohol
- Actions severe enough to warrant immediate dismissal
  - Stealing
  - Dealing drugs
  - Sleeping during work hours
  - Violence

Due Process

The right to due process means that an employer must follow a series of steps and document the results of these steps before terminating an employee. If these steps are not properly followed and proper documentation is not filed regarding the termination, the employee may be able to take legal action and either get his job back or receive a monetary settlement. If an employee is accused of a crime, such as theft, he is entitled to know what charges have been brought against him and must be given the right to fight the charges according to the law.

Guidelines regarding how an employee termination must be documented vary from state to state. It is important for a human resources manager to know what procedures and what types of documentation are necessary for employee termination.

Employment Law

Title VII of the Civil Rights Act

Title VII of the Civil Rights Act, passed in 1964, defines many issues that must be dealt with in the course of human resource management. These deal with discrimination, a problem that still exists in today's workforce.

Title VII of the Civil Rights Act states:

- No employer may refuse to hire, fail to hire, refuse to consider, or terminate an employee solely based on that employee's color, religion, race, gender or nationality.
- Specific classes of individuals are protected in regards to discriminatory practices.
- These classes are defined by race, gender, religion, disability, nationality and some other specific characteristics.
- The Equal Employment Opportunity Commission (EEOC) possesses authority to enforce these laws and regulations.

Americans with Disabilities Act (ADA)

Passed in 1990, the ADA specifically relates to practices regarding the employment of disabled individuals. Provisions of the ADA include:

- Definition of a disability.
- Lists of various disabilities covered by the act including:
    - Hearing or vision loss.
    - Reduced or impaired mobility.
    - Past history of cancer or heart disease.
    - Past history of mental illness.
    - Disfigurement.
    - Learning or developmental disabilities.
- Prohibition of discrimination in various areas including:
    - Promotions.
    - Termination.
    - Hiring.
    - Salary.
    - Benefits.
    - Layoffs.
- Requirement for accommodations for those suffering from disabilities, including access to the workplace and alternate assessment procedures.

This act has had a major effect on human resources management as companies work to fulfill its requirements and produce guidelines regarding the treatment of disabled individuals.

Age Discrimination and Employment Act (ADEA)

The Age Discrimination and Employment Act, designed to protect employees from age discrimination, was passed in 1967, with revisions made to the act in 1986. Focusing on employment candidates or existing employees over the age of forty, the ADEA provides regulations similar to those in the Civil Rights Act that prevent discrimination against protected classes. The ADEA is also enforced by the Equal Employment Opportunity Commission.

The ADEA became necessary because of age discrimination occurring under circumstances such as:

- Older employees being laid off to save money because they typically had higher salaries.
- Older employees avoided in the hiring process because they were more experienced and would require higher pay but work for the company for a shorter period of time.
- Avoiding or removing older employees because of potential higher benefits costs to the company.

Equal Pay Act

The Equal Pay Act was passed in 1963. Designed to address gender discrimination, this act requires companies to provide the same pay to women and men performing the same work. The law also defines the parameters of equality so that equal work may be objectively determined. For example, jobs with the same duties but different titles may not be assigned different salaries based on the gender of the persons doing those jobs. Employers also may not pay different salaries based on perceived need of one gender over the other—for example, paying a man more money based on the assumption that he must support his family and therefore "needs" the money more than a woman doing the same work.

Pregnancy Discrimination Act

The Pregnancy Discrimination Act was passed in 1979 and prevents discrimination against pregnant women. Actions that may not be taken against pregnant women under the Pregnancy Discrimination Act include:

- Refusing to hire a woman because she is pregnant.
- Refusing to promote a woman because she is pregnant.
- Dismissing a woman because of her pregnancy.
- Forcing a woman to stop working during pregnancy when she is still physically able to work.
- Preventing a woman from returning to her job after her maternity leave.

Discriminating against pregnant women in these ways as well as others can leave a company open to discrimination lawsuits. The human resources manager must ensure that company policies and procedures prevent this type of discrimination.

Family and Medical Leave Act

The Family and Medical Leave Act, passed in 1993, provides additions to the Pregnancy Discrimination Act, passed in 1979. Any company with over 50 employees must provide leave for employees after a child is born or adopted into the family. Leave must be at least twelve weeks. This kind of leave can also be requested to provide time to care for a seriously ill child, parent, spouse, or due to the employee being seriously ill. After the leave is over, the company must bring the employee back into the company in the same or a similar job position. The company is also required to pay health insurance benefits during leave. If the employee does not return to work after the leave, he or she might be required to reimburse the company for these expenses.

Regulations That Apply to Federal Contractors

Four other major regulations exist that apply specifically to contractors working for the federal government.

- Executive Order 11246. Requires organizations with federal contracts over $50,000 to provide affirmative action plans.
- Executive Order 11478. Requires organizations with federal contracts over $10,000 to hire solely on merit without considering race, gender, religion or other factors.
- Vocational Rehabilitation Act of 1973. Federal contractors with contracts over $2,500 annually must provide affirmative action plans for disabled employees.
- Vietnam Era Veterans' Readjustment Act of 1974. Requires affirmative action in hiring veterans of the Vietnam War.

The Executive Orders are enforced through the Office of Federal Contract Compliance Procedures (OFCCP), as is the Vietnam Era Veterans' Readjustment Act. The Vocational Rehabilitation Act is enforced by the Department of Labor.

How Equal Employment Opportunity Legislation Is Enforced

The Equal Employment Opportunity Commission (EEOC) and the Office of Federal Contract Compliance Procedures (OFCCP) are the two main agencies that enforce EEO legislation.

The EEOC is part of the Department of Justice. Its responsibilities are focused on enforcing Title VII of the Civil Rights Act, the Equal Pay Act, and the ADA. It investigates and manages discrimination complaints, collects information about US business trends and patterns regarding employment, and provides information about new guidelines.

The OFCCP audits government contractors to ensure their compliance with affirmative action requirements and requests cancellation or suspension of contracts, or even criminal action, if companies are not complying.

Fair Labor Standards Act (FLSA)

One of the older regulations affecting human resource managers, FLSA was passed in 1938. This landmark legislation established the minimum wage. The purpose of a minimum wage was to ensure that all workers in the US would receive wages enough to cover all basic needs. Over time, the minimum wage has been increased in response to increases in cost of living.

FLSA also established a standard workweek of 40 hours and defined guidelines for the payment of overtime if more than 40 hours is worked in a single seven-day period. It also included regulations controlling child labor.

Employee Retirement Income Security Act (ERISA)

ERISA was instituted in 1974 and helps protect employee pensions. Under ERISA, money employees invest in their retirement plans is protected, and at the time of retirement they are ensured access to certain pension benefits. They are also entitled to pension benefits if they are terminated. ERISA was intended to keep companies from misusing funds employees had placed into their retirement plans, as some companies were investing this money inappropriately, using it to fund company operations, or otherwise misusing the funds, leading to loss of money that technically belonged to employees.

Occupational Safety and Health Act (OSHA)

OSHA, passed in 1970, provides various regulations regarding workplace safety. It is administrated by the Department of Labor. In addition, the Department of Health works, through the National Institute for Occupational Safety and Health, to sponsor research to determine what these safety standards should be and how employees should be trained to ensure the standards and guidelines are properly followed. Companies that do not follow these regulations can be subject to large penalties or criminal prosecution. The Department of Labor conducts inspections at the workplace to be sure proper regulations are followed. Employees who request an inspection due to observed poor practice are protected with anonymity. In addition to safety guidelines, companies are also required to report fatal injuries or accidents.

Worker Adjustment and Retraining Notification (WARN) Act

Under the WARN Act, companies with 100 employees or more enacting a large-scale layoff (50 employees or more) or planning to close a particular facility must provide sufficient warning to those employees who will be affected. Sufficient warning is defined as at least sixty days. This warning period is meant to provide time for the employees to find another job. WARN also provides for warnings of significant work hour reduction. If the company does not provide sufficient notification, this lapse can result in major fines. Although WARN is intended to benefit employees, from the company's perspective, providing warning is not always in its best interests, as highly qualified workers are more likely to be able to find new jobs, thus removing their talents from the company pool. For the employee, though, WARN provides a much-needed grace period in which to find continuing employment.

Drug-Free Workplace Act

The Drug-Free Workplace Act of 1988 provides regulations meant to reduce illegal drug use in the workplace. It focuses largely on federal contractors and government employees, but also applies to jobs that fall under the regulatory eye of the Nuclear Regulatory Commission and the Department of Transportation. Some jobs, under these regulations, require employees to undergo drug testing on a regular basis.

Many companies not explicitly covered by the Drug-Free Workplace Act also follow the regulations defined by the act. These companies also require drug testing for employees. Controversy has arisen regarding whether this kind of testing constitutes an invasion of privacy.

Privacy Act

In 1974, the Privacy Act was passed, providing regulations regarding the privacy of federal employees. The main purpose of the act was to allow employees to review their own personnel records to ensure all information included was accurate. Limiting access to personnel files to managers or other administrative personnel is no longer legal under the provisions of this act.

Other privacy concerns also exist in the workplace that are not covered by the Privacy Act. These include an employer's access to an individual employee's e-mail correspondence, as well as the contents of an individual computer workstation. These issues require a sensible balance between a company's security concerns and an employee's right to privacy.

Patriot Act

The Patriot Act was enacted after September 11, 2001 and the terrorist attacks on the World Trade Center and the Pentagon. Intended to assist the government and law enforcement agencies in their efforts to reduce terrorism, it has raised many concerns about individual privacy. The provisions of the Patriot Act allow law enforcement agencies investigating possible terrorist activity to:

- Investigate individuals without notifying the individuals of the investigation.
- Use surveillance techniques to gather information.
- Share information among various agencies.
- Acquire business records, such as purchasing patterns, that previously would have been considered private.
- Obtain search warrants on the grounds that terrorist activities might have occurred at a certain location.

The Patriot Act was allowed to lapse in 2005, but was reinstated the next year.

Ethics

Ethics are important to any career, but are particularly applicable in the case of human resources management. In addition to following regulatory guidelines and laws governing the treatment of various employees, a human resources manager must consider the ethics of certain actions. In some cases, following the letter of the law is ethically unacceptable, and a compromise must be made. These decisions are often determined by corporate culture, traditions within the company, and company-specific guidelines.

Compliance with Regulations

Making sure a company is in compliance with relevant regulations is a three-step process.

1. Make sure managers clearly understand all laws and regulations that directly affect their relationship with their employees.
2. Ensure there is a qualified, knowledgeable human resources staff to help guide managers in these decisions as they arise.
3. Perform audits of company procedures related to human resource management. These audits are most effective if performed by an outside agency.

Following these steps will help ensure the company is on solid legal ground at all times with regards to how it treats and interacts with its employees.

National Labor Relations Act

The National Labor Relations Act (NLRA) is also known as the Wagner Act. It was passed in 1935 to address interaction between companies and labor unions. In effect, the act gave unions more power to negotiate for employee rights as well as regulating the negotiations themselves by providing guidelines for actions such as collective bargaining. It also provided guidelines and regulations for how a union could be formed and how organizations must interact with unions. The Wagner Act greatly increased the power of unions and led to rapidly increasing union membership.

Taft-Hartley Act

By 1947, several major labor strikes had changed the landscape of union/corporation relations. Feeling that the Wagner Act had shifted the balance of power too far to the side of the unions, the Taft-Hartley Act was passed to make the relationship more equal, which had been the intention of the Wagner Act. In addition, the Taft-Hartley Act included creation of a federal organization—the

National Labor Relations Board (NLRB)—to enforce the act. The Landrum-Griffin Act, passed in 1959, further addressed these concerns.

As regarded unions, the Taft-Hartley act outlawed closed shops, secondary boycotts, and jurisdictional strikes. It also allowed states to pass certain anti-union legislation. Both unions and management were no longer allowed to provide monetary support for federal candidates for office.

Civil Service Reform Act

The Civil Service Reform Act, passed in 1978, restructured regulations regarding the United States Civil Service. Most of its provisions are directly related to federal human resources management. Dismantling the US Civil Service Commission, the Civil Service Reform Act set up three new agencies:

1. Office of Personnel Management (OPM)—regulates and guides human resources in federal organizations.
2. Merit Systems Protection Board (MSPB)—deals with employees who have lost their jobs or undergone disciplinary procedures and wish to appeal these actions.
3. Federal Labor Relations Authority (FLRA)—provides regulations regarding federal employees' rights to form unions and make use of collective bargaining procedures.

COBRA

The Comprehensive Omnibus Budget Reconciliation Act (COBRA) requires companies with at least twenty employees to extend health insurance benefits for up to eighteen months after an employee leaves their job or is terminated or laid off. Employees may choose whether or not to pay the necessary premiums to receive this extended coverage. It also provides for health insurance coverage in other situations including:

- Work hours reduction.
- Time between jobs when coverage would otherwise be interrupted.
- Divorce that eliminates coverage for one involved partner.
- Death that eliminates coverage for a family member.

In addition, COBRA requires the company to provide the employee with sufficient notice of changes in employment that would make them eligible for COBRA benefits.

Electromation v. NLRB and E.I. DuPont de Nemours v. NLRB

Although the importance of unions in American corporations has decreased, two major cases have ensured that unions still maintain influence. These two cases deal largely with the corporation's right to form committees to oversee the relationship between management and labor.

- Electromation v. NLRB. In this case, the company involved formed "action committees" intended to address issues such as workplace conditions. The court ruled that the committees, made up mostly of management personnel, threatened the existing union.
- E.I. DuPont de Nemours v. NLRB. Similar to the Electromation case, this case also ruled that committees set up within the company—in this instance safety committees—could be defined as labor unions and, since they were dominated by management, violated the Taft-Hartley Act.

Labor Relations

Labor Relations

Labor relations refers to the relationship between unions and the companies employing individuals who belong to these unions. The interaction between employers and union employees is regulated by several federal laws, and when dealing with these employees, the human resources manager must bear in mind these laws so that the company is not found to be in violation. Companies also must deal with negotiations with unions from time to time, as well as actions taken against the companies during these negotiations, such as strikes, walk-outs or other work cessation used to pressure the companies to agree to union demands. In general, unions are on a decline in the US, but in some industries and in some areas of the country, their influence remains strong.

Labor Union

A labor union is an organization made up of employees with similar job functions working together to achieve similar goals. Unions began with employees working to improve working conditions and increase wages. They continue to address similar concerns, as well as issues regarding benefits. Unions make use of collective bargaining, strikes and other methods to protest treatment by corporations and to improve the overall conditions under which their members are required to work. Unions are protected by a series of federal regulations, and must provide certain information to the appropriate government agency in order to receive all the benefits of this legal protection.

In the eighteenth century, some industries had formed small organizations known as craft unions. An early example is the Journeyman Cordwainers society of Philadelphia, formed in 1794 to help shoemakers achieve higher pay and better working conditions. By the 1830s, national unions began to form. It was not until 1869, however, that a union achieved notable impact, when the Knights of Labor brought numerous skilled workers together. Unfortunately, their efforts to improve working conditions ended in violence.

The American Federation of Labor (AF of L) followed in 1886 and eventually joined with the Congress of Industrial Organization (CIO) to form the AFL-CIO in 1955. The efforts of unions have led to major improvements in working conditions in the US, but their influence had gradually faded in recent years.

Union Organizational Structure

Though individual unions have their own structures, most follow a general structural outline. Each union has an international union, which oversees a variety of local unions, which can cover a region, a company or even an individual plant. Local unions have a regional officer to coordinate efforts and administrative issues. The national union also has a president and its own executive board. Large unions also often have departments to manage different issues within the union, such as providing assistance to local unions or overseeing collective bargaining when it occurs. Within each local union, the shop steward acts as a liaison between the union and the corporation.

Developing Trends

In the past, unions fought for better pay for union employees, as well as better benefits. Sometimes these demands involved significant salary or wage increases in order to offset cost of living increases or to address other concerns.

As the economic climate has shifted, unions find themselves in a different position, with negotiations often focusing on other issues such as:

- Avoiding salary cuts.
- Maintaining job security.
- Maintaining benefits.
- Acquiring improved pension plans.
- Preventing companies from outsourcing work to other countries.

Though not as dramatic as increased wages and salaries, these goals still focus on maintaining or improving conditions for union employees.

Collective Bargaining

Collective bargaining refers to the process of negotiation between a union and the management of the corporation that employs the union members. The outcome of the collective bargaining process is a long-term agreement between the employer and the union members. These agreements typically are put into effect for a certain number of years, at which time the union might choose to renegotiate the terms of the agreement, leading to another collective bargaining process.

Preparing for Collective Bargaining

Collective bargaining can be a complex process that takes some time. Preparation can help reduce the amount of time it takes to come to an agreement, as well as reduce the possibility of a strike.

Management can prepare for collective bargaining in any or all of the following ways.

- Research types of agreements that exist in companies with similar profiles.
- Research types of agreements the specific union has made in the past.
- Evaluate the company's ability to increase wages or salaries or to meet other expected demands by the union.

The union can prepare by assembling similar information such as:

- Company financial records.
- Information about agreements reached by other companies.
- Information about contracts made between the company and other unions.

Setting Parameters for Collective Bargaining

Before collective bargaining begins, the union and the company involved must set parameters that will govern the session. These include defining mandatory items and permissive items.

Mandatory items include benefits, wages and salaries, and hours employees are expected to work. Either side in the negotiation can request that these issues be discussed, and the other is required to agree to the discussion.

Permissive items will only be brought to the bargaining table if both parties agree to discuss them.

Some items cannot be negotiated at all because of labor laws. For example, management cannot ask the union not to strike and include that in their contract with the company.

Bargaining Zone

As with any negotiation, parties from both sides meet at a specific time and location to discuss the issues agreed upon when parameters were set for the negotiation. Negotiation can be quick and simple or protracted and difficult. Some labor negotiations have literally gone on for years before an agreement was reached.

One important tool used by both sides during negotiation is the bargaining zone. Each side defines three points.

- The desired result.
- A result representing a reasonable expectation.
- The point at which demands become unreasonable to the other party.

Within the span of these possible results is the bargaining zone. Ideally, both sides will be able to come to an agreement that fits within the reasonable expectations of both sides, or which comes close to both sides' desired results.

Choosing to Unionize

In the early days of unions, employees unionized in order to protest unacceptable working conditions. As unions grew and became engrained in the workplace environment, workers in certain fields were expected to join unions. Employees followed these expectations in the belief that joining the union would be beneficial to them and provide better working conditions and compensation in the long run. Now, the choice to join a union is often influenced by factors including the specific industry, the area of the country, the influence of the union, and even family factors such as a history in the family of belonging to a specific union.

Administering Labor Agreements

An important part of the finalized labor contract is guidelines on how the contract will be administered within the company. The more objective and clear-cut these guidelines are, the less likely it is that problems will come up later regarding interpretation and administration.

An example of a guideline regarding how a contract is administered could involve how disputes are handled, or exactly how wage increases will be granted and over what period of time. Some issues can be easily managed with clear-cut guidelines, while others might require a union official such as a shop steward to assist with decisions on a case-by-case basis.

Differences in Employee Rights Between Unionized and Non-Unionized Work Settings

Unions originally came about in order to ensure employee rights and to secure better compensation and better working conditions. Since then, many of these issues have been addressed by federal legislation, making many of the rights unions fought for available to any employee in any setting.

In a unionized setting, additional workplace issues are dealt with through the union hierarchy. If an employee feels slighted or mistreated, he can request help from union officials to make his case. In a non-unionized setting, an employee can bring grievances to the human resources department or, if necessary, to a court of law. Both workplace environments provide a wide range of protection for employees.

International Human Resources Management

Human Resource Management Strategies for International Corporations

When dealing with international human resource management, international corporations must decide on a specific strategy. Three common strategies are:

1. Ethnocentric staffing model. Personnel from the country where the main office is located are used to staff executive positions in foreign offices in order to maintain the perspective of the home office.
2. Polycentric staffing model. Executive positions in foreign offices are staffed largely by natives of the country where those offices are located. In this strategy, the company believes that these employees are better able to interpret and respond to local market issues.
3. Geocentric staffing model. In this case, the best employee is chosen for the job regardless of where they are from.

Ethnocentric, Polycentric and Geocentric Staffing Models

For each approach to international staffing models, the human resource manager will face a slightly different set of challenges.

1. Ethnocentric staffing model. Human resources will focus on training managers, compensation issues for out-of-country positions, and managing moves both out of the country and back to the home country.
2. Polycentric staffing model. Human resources concerns will include establishing local HR departments in the host countries and coordinating these with the home country's HR department.

Geocentric staffing model. HR must consider international issues in every aspect of HR function from selection to planning to training. Satellite locations will also have individual HR departments

Cultural Environment

When cultural differences between a home office and international satellite offices are significant, they can have a dramatic effect on how business is done. Human resources managers must be aware of different customs, beliefs and language issues that could lead to miscommunication and other difficulties and challenges in the host countries. Some of these issues can include:

- Roles of women.
- Relationship between management and subordinates.
- Acceptability of child labor.
- Specific business practices.
- Different wages and standards of living.

All of these issues can lead to various challenges when dealing with human resource management in other countries.

Political and Legal Environments

The political climate of another country can also have a major effect on how business is done in that country. Four major areas involving political and legal issues must be considered when doing business internationally.

1. Stability of the local government. The government itself may be unstable, or it may be subject to frequent changes in its attitudes and policies toward foreign business interests.
2. International trade controls. Some countries enforce tariffs or quotas to control how much international trade can take place within their borders. This can include requirements regarding hiring of local employees.
3. International trade incentives. Some countries offer incentives such as tax breaks to foreign interests in order to attract their business.
4. Economic communities. When different countries make agreements, these agreements often include guidelines regarding foreign business interests. The European Union (EU) is an example of an economic community.

Issues That Must Be Addressed

In general, there are four major areas international human resource managers must address:

1. Training and development. Employees in other countries might not have the same basic education expected from American employees. In addition, special training must be supplied for executives chosen to work in other countries.
2. Working conditions. Compensation for executives moving to other countries must be commensurate with the cost of living in that country, and the standard of living must also be maintained.
3. Employee sourcing. HR managers must determine whether employees should be recruited from the local population, the population of the home country, or another source altogether.
4. Legal and cultural conflicts. Companies in the US must follow certain guidelines, but these guidelines may not be supported or might even be contradicted in other countries.

Exporting and Licensing, Direct Foreign Investments and Joint Ventures

As in domestic companies, an international company's corporate strategy can affect the human resource strategies employed. Some examples include:

- Exporting or licensing. In this corporate strategy, the company simply exports goods to another country or allows another company to manufacture the parent company's goods in another country. These approaches to international business do not have a large effect on human resource management strategy.
- Direct foreign investment. The parent company owns a physical facility in another country. In these cases, HR must respond to staffing needs in the foreign country.
- Strategic alliance or joint venture. Several companies work together to form a partnership. HR strategy can differ depending upon the parameters of the alliance, and could involve coordination among several HR departments.

Recruiting and Selection

According to the company's strategic plan, HR will recruit either from the home country, the satellite country or another source. In any case, the HR department must have a plan in place for recruitment and selection that follows legal guidelines of the host country and also meets the needs of the parent company. The training strategy must consider similar issues, such as the level of training that will be necessary and how to manage language issues. Compensation can also be complex, since a host country might have a vastly different standard of living than the parent country. Achieving a balance in these areas is a complex undertaking, and must be considered by the human resource management department of any international corporation.

Expatriates

An employee who is sent to work in another country is referred to as an expatriate. Selecting the right employees to assign to these jobs is another challenge faced by the human resources department. Individuals sent to work in foreign locations must have not only the necessary skills to do the work required at that position, but must also be able to function and work efficiently in a foreign country. The recruiting and selection process must take this into account. Training must be administered to prepare the expatriate not only for job duties, but for the specific demands and hardships of working in a foreign location. Compensation guidelines will also take into account the difficulty of this type of assignment, often factoring a hardship premium or foreign-service premium into the employee's salary.

Challenges

Labor relations in foreign countries can be much more complex than those in the United States. While unions are on a decline in the US, they are on the rise in other countries where employees are still working to improve their conditions. Labor unions in other countries are often much more focused on social issues, as well. In order to function efficiently in an international setting, the international human resource manager must understand the role of labor unions in host countries as well as traditional expectations regarding how unions interact with management and the overall attitude toward contracts between unions and corporations.

Current Issues and Trends

Diversity

Diversity in the workplace involves the overall makeup of the workforce. Affirmative action brings more employees of protected classes into the mix, and the natural dynamics of the surrounding population will also affect the makeup of the workforce. Diversity can be defined according to several dimensions including age, gender, national origin, race, and disability.

Current trends see the average workplace incorporating more diversity. This is due to the effects of affirmative action and other regulations as well as changes taking place in the selection pool overall. More qualified women and minorities are available in the general population as they have experienced greater access to education and other deciding factors. Globalization is another trend that has increased overall diversity in the American workforce.

There are several major dimensions of diversity in the American workplace.

- Gender. Over the past several decades, more women have entered the workforce, so that almost half the workforce is currently made up of women.
- Age. More people are choosing to work longer, and changes in mandatory retirement age have also led to a larger number of older workers.
- Ethnicity. Changes in the overall ethnic composition of the US have led to ethnic diversity in the workplace, especially as regards Hispanic Americans.
- Disability. More disabled workers have entered the work force due to legislation and increased efforts to provide assistance so they can efficiently perform their jobs.

Diversity in the workforce provides a variety of advantages to the company, but also can lead to negative results if it is not properly handled. Positive effects of diversity on an organization include:

- Social change. The increasing diversity of the workplace has led to changes in how people interact with diverse populations outside the workplace.
- Competitive advantage. A diverse workforce provides a larger pool of knowledge and creativity, as well as direct understanding of minority groups to which products are marketed. Diversity management can also make a company more flexible, and can make a company more appealing to highly qualified candidates in minority classes, thus increasing overall competitive advantage.

If a company does not handle diversity well—a task that falls largely upon the human resources department—conflict could arise in the workforce. Conflict regarding diversity often arises from the belief that protected classes are given preferential treatment.

Diversity Management and Equal Employment Opportunity (EEO)

While EEO prevents discrimination based on an employee's differences, and provides specific guidelines regarding certain protected classes, diversity management focuses more on assisting diverse employees in the performance of their jobs. EEO seeks to reduce the impact of differences to provide equitable rewards regardless of diversity. Diversity management acknowledges differences between individuals and works to accommodate those differences. Diversity management from a human resources perspective requires companies to accommodate different needs based on gender, religion or disability, such as additional days off for non-Christian religious holidays, maternity leave, and tools to help disabled employees perform their jobs.

Strategies for Diversity Management

There are several strategies for diversity management, some of which are more applicable to individuals, while others apply to the organization as a whole. On an individual level, strategies include:

- Open communication.
- Understanding of what diversity means.
- Empathy toward others.
- Tolerating cultural differences.

On an organizational level, important strategies include:

- Corporate policy regarding diversity.
- Corporate practice regarding diversity.
- Training specifically designed to address diversity issues.
- Overall corporate culture.

By putting policies and practice into effect that help manage diversity issues, instituting diversity training, and maintaining a corporate culture that supports diverse employees, the organization can set the standard for diversity management.

Information Technology

Information technology is any approach or system a company uses to manage its information. Information can be managed manually or with computers. The latter has become much more common in recent years.

An information technology (IT) system consists of the following basic elements.

- Input medium—tool that allows information to be input into the system, e.g. a keyboard or scanner.
- Processor—tool that organizes, sorts or otherwise manipulates the data, such as a spreadsheet program.
- Storage device—tool or place where data is stored, such as a hard drive or even a file cabinet.
- Output medium—means by which data is transformed into usable information, such as a printer.
- Control system—system that controls the overall process, usually software in today's IT environment.

Human Resource Information System

A human resource information system (HRIS) is simply an information system constructed specifically to manage human resource related information and data. This includes not only software or filing systems but also the specific necessary information and the personnel required to distribute and analyze that information.

The requirements of a specific HRIS depend upon the needs of the organization itself. Some companies use specialized packages to manage their HRIS needs, while others develop an effective HRIS in-house. Most HRISs in modern corporations are computerized, eliminating the need for extensive paperwork and filing.

The specific uses of the HRIS in a corporation depends upon its organizational needs, but in general the HRIS is used to support all human resources management efforts. These tasks can include:

- Posting job openings.
- Maintaining performance appraisal records.
- Keeping an ongoing history of employees' training and development.
- Maintaining information regarding wages, salaries and benefits.
- Keeping records regarding an employee's career path.
- Maintaining personal information regarding individual employees for easy access and retrieval.
- General record keeping duties.
- Report generation.

Record keeping and report generation are the most common uses for an HRIS. Human resource departments can keep track of benefits, compensation and various details about how these are administered relatively easily using an efficient HRIS. They can also easily generate reports to meet the needs of various administrators within the company.

An HRIS typically stores a wide range of information about individual employees, much of which could be considered personal or private. In turn, this information is often widely available to those with access to the HRIS, and the employee has very little control over who can access this information and how it is used. Thus the majority of concerns that arise surrounding HRISs in corporations involve the potential invasion of privacy. The 1974 Privacy Act placed restrictions on how federal organizations could use this type of information, but no similar legislation exists regarding private companies. The Privacy Protection Study Commission has issued a series of recommendations regarding employee rights, but the appropriate balance between the employee's right to privacy and the corporation's ability to use information for decision-making has yet to be determined.

Virtual Office

The virtual office has become more and more common in today's corporations. In these cases, employees do not necessarily work at a specific location, such as company headquarters, but work out of satellite offices or out of their own homes. Use of the Internet and telephone enables them to interact with other employees or with clients. Employees can even access the company databases from a remote location using special software. Using virtual offices reduces many company expenses involved in maintaining a large building, but can also raise issues of liability and overall productivity, especially if employees are working out of their homes. This practice can also be referred to as telecommuting.

Contingent Workers

A contingent worker is a worker hired on for the short-term to take on a specific task. When this task is completed, the worker is let go. Typically, these types of workers are temporary employees, such as office staff, or contractors with specialized skills for the task that needs to be completed. Contingent workers are often employed through another agency that places them with companies as they are needed. Part-time workers, independent contractors and on-call workers fall into the category of contingent workers. Contingent workers enable a company to be more flexible, but in some cases can lead to decreased productivity and/or a lack of employees with a long-term investment in the company.

AUTONOMOUS WORK GROUPS

An autonomous work group is a group of employees working together on a specific project. Rather than being assigned duties by an outside supervisor, these groups often assign duties to individual members within the group itself. The groups work independently of other employees or groups within the organization, making use of specialized skills and knowledge to achieve a particular goal. Human resource issues regarding assessment, compensation and supervisory tasks can arise regarding autonomous work groups, especially if these issues are not clearly defined before the group comes into existence.

DSST Practice Test

Want to take this practice test in an online interactive format?
Check out the online resources page, which includes interactive practice questions and much more: **mometrix.com/resources719/dssthumresman**

1. Which of the following is correct about branding relative to human resources?

a. Branding applies to marketing and sales, but not to human resource management.
b. Branding has to do with a company's corporate image or culture in terms of HR.
c. Branding means that some corporations have a brand, but other companies don't.
d. Branding identifies a firm's public reputation but has little to do with employees.
e. Branding in employment is completely separate from product or business brands.

2. Of the following areas, which is not considered a function of human resource management?

a. Staffing
b. Development
c. Compensation
d. Human capital metrics
e. Employee and labor relations

3. Joe, a middle manager in a corporation, tends to agree with his boss and with other corporate leaders in general about what is right or wrong in hiring and management practices and his actions at work tend to be consistent with his beliefs. This description of Joe is an example of:

a. Type I ethics
b. Type II ethics
c. Types I and II ethics
d. Type III ethics
e. None of these

4. Which of the following is not one of the steps in organizational strategic planning?

a. Mission determination
b. Environmental assessment
c. Objective establishment
d. Strategy determination
e. Strategy implementation

Use the following information to answer Question 5:

> Job analysis is meant to answer six main questions. Two of these questions are: What physical and mental tasks does the employee do? *and:* What qualifications are required to do the job?

5. Which is not one of the other four questions?

a. What tools does the employee use?
b. When should the job be completed?
c. Where is this job going to be done?
d. How does the employee do the job?
e. For what reason(s) is this job done?

6. One method used by job analysts is observation of employees. Which of these is not another method used in job analysis?

a. Interviews
b. Questionnaires
c. Employee recording
d. Combining methods
e. Social media sites

7. Which of these is not considered an alternative to recruitment for an organization?

a. Overtime
b. Outsourcing
c. Contingent workers
d. Promotion from within
e. Professional employer organizations

8. According to the Department of Labor's 2006 guidelines for online recruiting, which is not a criterion to determine if someone is an Internet applicant?

a. The individual has applied for a specific job on the company's website.
b. The individual is considered only for a certain open job by the employer.
c. The individual applies during a time with high labor market conditions.
d. The individual finds s/he meets the job's stated minimum qualifications.
e. The individual has not subsequently rescinded his/her interest in the job.

9. Which of these is not true of environmental variables that impact the employee selection process?

a. The time that a company has to make hiring decisions has a great impact on the process.
b. The level of a job in the company's hierarchy has no effect on its approach to selection.
c. The size of the applicant pool and resulting selection ratio change the selection process.
d. The type of organization involved in the selection process differentially affects choices.
e. The use of a period of probation can replace part of the selection process or evaluate it.

10. Of the following required characteristics of well-designed job selection tests, which is the most important?

a. Validity
b. Reliability
c. Test norms
d. Objectivity
e. Standardization

11. Which of these would not be a measure a company could take when anticipating a shortage of workers?

a. Offering flexible work hours
b. Offering training programs
c. Raising selection standards
d. Seeking different applicants
e. Looking for applicants in different places

12. If a firm anticipates having an excess of workers, which of the following is less likely than the others to be a measure it would take to address this problem?

a. Restricted hiring
b. Early retirement
c. Reduced hours
d. Outsourcing
e. Downsizing

13. What is the correct definition of outplacement?

a. Outplacement is another term for the practice of outsourcing
b. Outplacement is employment assistance for laid-off workers
c. Outplacement is assigning employees to work in other places
d. Outplacement is placing employees with cooperating firms.
e. Outplacement is providing for filling vacated high positions

14. Factors interacting with training and development include (1) the success of other HR functions and (2) the support of upper management leaders. Which of the following is not one of several other factors interacting with training and development?

a. Involvement and commitment of both generalist and specialist management
b. Technological progress in how knowledge is delivered and business is done
c. Multilevel firm structures and more complex worker tasks and interactions
d. Variations in learning styles, including relevance, timing and types of activities
e. These are all factors that interact with training and development and affect its delivery processes

15. Which of the following is not a basic reason for conducting regular orientation at a company?

a. To do management development training
b. To acquaint workers with the firm culture
c. To give access to developmental programs
d. To integrate workers via socializing them
e. To reiterate the value of team membership

16. Of the following training and development methods, which is least likely to involve a classroom and instructor?

a. Case study method
b. Apprenticeships
c. Job rotation
d. Internships
e. Blended

17. Which of these is not a special training area for supervisors and employees?

a. ESL
b. Ethics
c. Remedial
d. Onboarding
e. Anger management

18. Of the following, which is not one of the levels in the Kirkpatrick Model of training evaluation?

a. Benchmarking
b. Extent of learning
c. Behavioral change
d. Participant opinions
e. Objectives achieved

19. Which of these types of career paths involves any vertical movement?

a. A dual-career path
b. A network career path
c. A lateral skill path
d. All of these paths do
e. None of these paths do

20. What is not a tool typically used in career planning?

a. The use of self-assessment
b. A strength/weakness balance sheet
c. A likes and dislikes survey
d. None of these would be tools used
e. All of these tools are used for career planning

21. Uses of performance appraisals include HR planning for promotions; predicting job performance of applicants for recruitment and selection; and identifying an employee's needs for training and development. Of the following, which is not an additional use or purpose of performance appraisal?

a. To aid career planning/development
b. To reward or to punish an employee
c. To facilitate compensation decisions
d. To aid decisions in internal relations
e. To assess potential for different jobs

22. In performance appraisal, halo error is to horn error as:

a. Appraiser discomfort is to employee anxiety
b. Lack of objectivity is to recent behavior bias
c. Leniency in ratings is to strictness in ratings
d. Recent behavior bias is to stereotyping bias
e. Manipulating the system is to personal bias

23. Which of these performance appraisal methods uses the largest number of sources for feedback?

a. The critical incident method
b. The essay method
c. The forced distribution method
d. The 720-degree review method
e. The 360-degree feedback method

24. How does the Behaviorally Anchored Rating Scales (BARS) method compare to rating scales methods of performance appraisal?

a. The BARS method uses specific examples of actions for each rating category.
b. The BARS method has more rating categories, and this is the only difference.
c. The BARS method is simply one specific kind of rating scale that has a name.
d. The BARS method employs fewer rating categories than rating scales employ.
e. The BARS method uses a bar graph to show how each ability has been rated.

25. In equity theory, which of these is the correct definition of internal equity?

a. Employees are paid similarly to employees doing similar jobs in other companies.
b. Those doing similar jobs in the same firm are paid according to individual factors.
c. Employees in a work group or team are compensated based on the group's success.
d. This is a perception by firms and individuals of fairness in payment for employees.
e. Employees are paid based on the relative importance of their job in the same firm.

26. Of the following methods of job evaluation, which one is not a fifth distinct method but a variation of one of the other four methods?

a. The point method
b. The ranking method
c. The Hay Plan method
d. The classification method
e. The factor comparison method

27. If a company pays an employee a bonus, that bonus is a type of:

a. Merit pay
b. Variable pay
c. Piecework pay
d. Skill-based pay
e. Competency-based pay

28. Collapsing many salary grades into a few groups containing a wide range of jobs is called:

a. Broadbanding
b. Pay ranges
c. Wage curves
d. Single-rate system
e. Adjusting pay rates

29. Of the following, which is not a legally required employee benefit?

a. Social Security
b. Workers' compensation
c. Family and medical leave
d. Payment for time not worked
e. Unemployment compensation

30. Which of these is not considered a discretionary employee benefit?

a. Health insurance
b. Life insurance
c. Retirement plan
d. Disability plan
e. All of these

31. Since the Occupational Safety and Health Administration (OSHA) was formed in 1970, its work has:

a. cut deaths at work by 30% and job injuries/illnesses by 10%.
b. cut deaths at work by 40% and job injuries/illnesses by 20%.
c. cut deaths at work by 50% and job injuries/illnesses by 30%.
d. cut deaths at work by 60% and job injuries/illnesses by 40%.
e. cut deaths at work by 70% and job injuries/illnesses by 50%.

32. The National Institute of Occupational Safety and Health (NIOSH) has ranked 130 jobs in terms of how stressful they are. Which of the following is not one of the 12 most stressful jobs according to this ranking?

a. Secretary
b. Waitress
c. Professor
d. Lab technician
e. Office manager

33. Which of the following is not true regarding workplace safety programs?

a. Conducting a job hazard analysis can make a job or task safer.
b. Before OSHA, almost no companies had good safety programs.
c. Compliance with Superfund Amendments and Reauthorization Act (SARA) would end most OSHA violations.
d. Involving employees in safety programs enhances the programs.
e. Designating a safety engineer can improve a company's safety.

34. According to the Hot Stove Rule approach, which of these is not a consequence that disciplinary action in a workplace should have?

a. Warning
b. Immediacy
c. Consistency
d. Impersonality
e. Progressiveness

35. What answer arranges the following equal employment opportunity legislation in the correct chronological order from earliest to latest? (Note: This refers to the initial passage of each law, not to any subsequent amendments.)

a. The Civil Rights Act; the Equal Pay Act; the Age Discrimination in Employment Act; the Pregnancy Discrimination Act; the Americans with Disabilities Act
b. The Equal Pay Act; the Civil Rights Act; the Americans with Disabilities Act; the Pregnancy Discrimination Act; the Age Discrimination in Employment Act
c. The Americans with Disabilities Act; the Civil Rights Act; the Pregnancy Discrimination Act; the Equal Pay Act; the Age Discrimination in Employment Act
d. The Age Discrimination in Employment Act; the Civil Rights Act; the Americans with Disabilities Act; the Pregnancy Discrimination Act; the Equal Pay Act
e. The Pregnancy Discrimination Act; the Equal Pay Act; the Civil Rights Act; the Americans with Disabilities Act; the Age Discrimination in Employment Act

36. In passing the Civil Rights Act of 1991, Congress amended the Civil Rights Act of 1866. It also amended four other laws. Which of the following was not one of those so amended?

a. Title VII of the 1964 Civil Rights Act
b. The Rehabilitation Act
c. The Immigration Reform and Control Act
d. The Age Discrimination in Employment Act
e. The Americans with Disabilities Act

37. Which of these was the first US law to address minimum wages?

a. The Walsh-Healy Act
b. The Davis-Bacon Act
c. Fair Labor Standards Act
d. The Equal Pay Act
e. The Civil Rights Act

38. According to the Fair Labor Standards Act (FLSA), which of the following is not considered an exempt employee from the law's overtime provisions?

a. Executives
b. Administrators
c. Professionals
d. Inside sales
e. Outside sales

39. Among the following health care laws, which one includes protections for the self-employed, for those with pre-existing medical conditions, and for the privacy of personal health information?

a. HIPAA
b. COBRA
c. ERISA
d. OWBPA
e. PPA

40. According to OSHA, an employee has the legal right of refusing to work under all except which one of these conditions?

a. The worker is afraid, with reason, of death, illness, or serious physical injury.
b. Serious harm to the worker is likely to happen immediately or in a short time.
c. Not enough time is available to file a complaint with OSHA and have it fixed.
d. The worker informed the employer and asked for resolution with no response.
e. Harm is not imminent but the worker wants to wait until there is a resolution.

41. The National Safe Workplace Institute has identified certain characteristics associated with businesses at high risk for workplace violence. Which of these is not one of those characteristics?

a. Frequent use of dangerous or potentially hazardous machinery
b. Frequent use of the grievance filing procedure by the workers
c. Frequent disputes between labor and management in the firm
d. Frequent workers' compensation claims for emotional injuries
e. Frequent insistence on overtime and lack of adequate staffing

42. Among many reasons that workers or former workers act violently against a business, which of these is not one of the most common reasons?

a. The business has fired/laid off employees
b. Marital problems and/or family problems
c. Alcohol or drug abuse by the employee(s)
d. Workers suffer from major mental illness
e. Personality conflicts among the personnel

43. Of the following types of employees, which is at relatively lesser risk of being a victim of workplace violence than the others?

a. A liquor store employee working alone
b. A bank teller on day shift with full staff
c. A driver of a taxi cab in an urban region
d. A delivery driver for a pizza restaurant
e. A police officer working the night shift

44. Which of the following is true regarding the issue of identity theft in the workplace?

a. The law making identity theft a federal crime was passed by Congress in 2000.
b. The FACTA of 2003 requires sensitive consumer information to be destroyed.
c. The FACTA was passed as a response to the FTC's passing its Disposal Rule.
d. Since several laws have outlawed and police it, identity theft is not a problem.
e. FACTA focuses on information for employment, credit, insurance, and others.

45. What is a correct statement about legislation concerning unions and the "closed shop?"

a. The Taft-Hartley Act legalized the closed shop for labor unions.
b. The Landrum-Griffin Act legalized the closed shop for unions.
c. The Landrum-Griffin Act allows closed shops in construction.
d. The Taft-Hartley Act allows closed shops for construction.
e. The Landrum-Griffin Act outlawed having closed shops.

46. Which of these is a management strategy for dealing with breakdowns in negotiations during the collective bargaining process?

a. Going on strike
b. Agreeing to a boycott
c. Informational picketing
d. Attempting secondary boycotts
e. Conducting a workplace lockout

47. In international companies with global staffing, which type of employees is usually the most common?

a. Third-country national employees
b. Expatriate employees
c. Neither (a) nor (b) is most common
d. Host-country national employees
e. (a) and (b) are both most common

48. Which kind of global staffing hires mainly expatriates as upper management in foreign locations?

a. Geocentric staffing
b. Polycentric staffing
c. Ethnocentric staffing
d. Regiocentric staffing
e. All of these kinds do.

49. A human resource information system (HRIS) should be timely, i.e., the information it provides to managers should be up-to-date. A good HRIS should also be all of these, except:

a. Accurate
b. Complex
c. Concise
d. Relevant
e. Complete

50. Regarding diversity in the workplace, which of the following is not a projection of coming trends?

a. The Department of Labor projects that by 2013, workers will outnumber jobs available.
b. The Bureau of Labor Statistics estimates the median age of workers as over 40 in 2010.
c. The Bureau of Labor Statistics estimates women will be 48% of the workforce in 2010.
d. The Bureau of Labor Statistics estimates women will be 59% of new workers in 2010.
e. According to current estimates, more than 70 million baby boomers will be 65 by year 2023.

Answer Key and Explanations

1. B	11. C	21. B	31. D	41. A
2. D	12. D	22. C	32. C	42. D
3. C	13. B	23. D	33. B	43. B
4. E	14. E	24. A	34. E	44. E
5. A	15. A	25. E	35. A	45. C
6. E	16. C	26. C	36. C	46. E
7. D	17. D	27. B	37. B	47. D
8. C	18. A	28. A	38. D	48. C
9. B	19. B	29. D	39. A	49. B
10. A	20. E	30. E	40. E	50. A

1. B: Branding (b) has to do with a company's corporate image or culture in terms of HR. Although historically, branding was more associated with marketing or sales (a), with so much competition among today's private enterprises for employees with valued abilities, it has become increasingly necessary for HR to develop its own most appropriate brand. It is not correct that (c) only some companies have a brand; according to HR experts, "Every company has a brand" (Joel Head, Headwinds Ltd.). While branding does identify a company's public reputation, it is not correct that branding has little to do with employees (d). In fact, HR brands do much to help firms attract the kinds of applicants for employment they want and need. Brands give applicants an idea of a particular company's culture and thus an idea of whether they want to work there. Branding in employment is not completely separate from product brands or business brands (e); rather, it is considered to be an extension of product or business branding.

2. D: Human capital metrics (d) are not considered a function of HR development but are rather measures of the effectiveness of HR performance. The five functional areas of HR management are staffing (a); HR development (b); compensation (c); safety and health (not listed as an answer choice in this question); and employee and labor relations (e).

3. C: This description is an example of (c) both Type I and Type II ethics. Type I ethics is defined as how strongly a person's moral beliefs correlate with the beliefs of existing sources of moral direction. Type II ethics is defined as how strongly a person's actions correlate with that person's beliefs. Joe's tendency to agree with his boss and with corporate leadership in general about right and wrong is an example of Type I ethics. Joe's tendency to act consistently with his beliefs at work is an example of Type II ethics. Because this example represents both Type I and Type II (c), Type I ethics only (a) is incorrect, as is Type II ethics only (b). There is no such thing in HRM known as Type III ethics (d). Because (c) is correct, answer (e), none of these, is incorrect.

4. E: Strategy implementation (e) is not one of the steps of strategic planning proper; it is a part of strategic management rather than planning. It takes place following the planning. It is often regarded as the most important part of strategic management because no matter how good the plan is, it will not succeed if not effectively implemented. The four steps of strategic planning in an organization are determining the corporate mission (a); assessment of the organization and its corporate environment (b), including both internal and external factors; the development of attainable, measurable corporate objectives (c) to be met; and arriving at strategies (d) to be used to reach the specified objectives.

5. A: What tools does the employee use (a) in the job is not one of the six main questions to be answered through job analysis. The answer to this question is rather one of the types of specific data collected through job analysis. The other four questions are: When is this job supposed to be completed? (b); Where should this job be done? (c); How does the employee do the job? (d); and For what reason(s) is this job done? (e).

6. E: Social media sites (e) are not used by job analysts for performing a job analysis. All of the other options are used by job analysts. The analyst may interview (a) the employee and the employee's supervisor separately. The analyst may also give structured questionnaires (b) to employees. Drawbacks to the use of this method alone include inadequate literacy in some employees and exaggeration of duties by some employees. Analysts may in some cases have certain types of workers do self-recording (c) of daily work duties in a log. Though this method is also prey to exaggeration by some workers, it is also useful for understanding the activities involved in performing very specialized positions. Since none of these methods is usually sufficient alone, job analysts most often combine methods (d) in conducting a job analysis, choosing those most appropriate to the particular job.

7. D: Promotion from within (d) is not considered as an alternative to recruitment but rather as one source of recruitment itself. Sources may be internal or external; promotion within the company is an internal source in the recruitment process. Because recruitment incurs a significant cost per hire, companies are advised to consider alternatives before recruiting new employees. Such alternatives include overtime (a) work for existing employees because the additional pay may in some cases be less than the cost of recruitment, selection, and training; outsourcing (b) of subcontractors to perform certain services when this is more effective and efficient; the use of contingent workers (c) including independent contractors and on-call workers who only work as needed, and temporary or short-term workers, which reduces employer expenses and addresses fluctuating work demands as well as needs for specialized skill sets; and the use of professional employer organizations (e) that lease employees to other businesses, freeing those other businesses from the administrative costs that become the PEO's responsibility.

8. C: Applying for a job during a time with high labor market conditions (c) is not a criterion of the DOL's 2006 online recruitment guidelines. Applying during a time with low labor market conditions would not be a criterion, either. The supply-to-demand ratio in the labor market for any given job skills at any given time is not related to the criteria for determining Internet applicants. The four criteria involved are (a) that the person has applied for a specific job on the company's website; (b) that the company is considering the applicant for only a certain position it has open, and if the applicant does not meet the qualifications specified in the job description for that position, the company is not required to consider the application; (d) the applicant finds from the job requirements that s/he has the minimum experience and/or training specified and expresses this in applying; and (e) the applicant has not later stated that s/he is no longer interested in the job for which s/he previously applied.

9. B: It is not true that (b) the level of a job in the company hierarchy will have no effect on approaches to selection. For example, the selection of a high-level executive will probably involve a much more lengthy and detailed process than would the selection of an entry-level clerical worker. It is true that the amount of time allowed for selection makes a difference (a). On one hand, research finds that quicker hiring by companies correlates strongly with higher overall return to their stockholders. On the other hand, searches for high-level executives, especially if they are made on a national or even international level, can take a long time. Bureaucratic organizations also have reputations for having lengthy selection processes. The situation also has an impact; for example, if a company cannot function without filling certain vacant positions, the time taken by the selection process may be drastically shortened by such an emergency. It is true that the applicant pool's size and the resulting selection ratio will change the process (c). If fewer qualified applicants exist than is optimal, the process becomes less selective because employers must choose from those available. If many well-qualified applicants exist, the process may be prolonged as employers try to narrow their choices down to the best candidate among several. Rates of unemployment have an effect on the selection ratio in that high unemployment is likely to assure more qualified applicants and low unemployment is likely to assure fewer qualified applicants. The type of organization does make a difference in the selection process (d). For example, in private-sector jobs, the ability of the applicant to help the company secure profits will be an important consideration; in government civil service systems, a manager may not get to interview any applicants except the few who scored highest on the system's competitive examination; and in nonprofit organizations, which often can only afford less competitive salaries, an applicant's commitment to the organization's mission may be considered equally with that applicant's job qualifications. Probationary periods in some companies (e) are used both as replacements for some parts of the selection process, in that if the newly-hired employee performs well in the position, other means of selection are unnecessary; and to evaluate the selection process, in that post-hiring monitoring of the new employee can reveal whether the decision to hire was valid.

10. A: All of the answer choices are required of adequately designed selection tests, but the most important is validity (a). The test must be able to show the test-taker's ability to do the job. This is the job-related definition of validity. In broader statistical terms, validity is defined as whether a test measures what it purports to measure. Good selection tests must also be reliable (b), meaning they are consistent over repeated administrations. They must have norms (c) to which their scores can be compared for reference, to see where a score falls within a normal distribution of a large sample. Selection tests must be objective (d), meaning all tests can be scored with the same results. For example, multiple-choice tests (such as this one) or true–false tests are objective tests because the same right or wrong answers must be chosen, while essay tests are not objective because there can be as many different answers as there are test-takers. Selection tests must also be standardized (e), meaning that the conditions under which the tests are administered must be uniform. The amount of time allotted to take the test and the instructions given must be the same in each administration. So should the environmental conditions be similar; i.e., one test administration should not be in a quiet, well-lighted room while another test administration is in a noisy, dark room because the results are likely to be different if so.

11. C: When anticipating an employee shortage, one thing that would not be a measure for a company to take would be (c) raising selection standards. In the face of a shortfall of workers, if anything the company might choose to lower its standards for selection. For example, a company that also chooses to implement a training program (b) to ensure an adequate supply of employees might require much less previous work experience in the same field (or none in some cases) and then train its new hires. Compensation incentives are another measure; these include (a) offering flexible work hours to attract employees with other responsibilities affecting their schedules, such as parenting, caregiving, attending school, or other employment. Other compensation incentives include shorter work weeks, the opportunity to telecommute, higher pay, and having child care centers on the work site. Other measures to address a shortage of workers might include considering different types of applicants (d) than the company has before, and recruiting in different geographical areas (e) than where it has previously looked.

12. D: A firm anticipating too many workers would be less likely to engage in (d) outsourcing to address the situation than in the other choices given. Outsourcing is a way to gain employees that can be more efficient and reduce labor costs, but would do nothing to address a surfeit of employees (unless the outsourcing accompanied the elimination of an equal number of local employees who were paid more and/or received more employee benefits than the outsourced workers, or it accompanied the elimination of a larger number of local employees than outsourced workers). Restricted hiring (a) would be one way to address a worker surplus: Employees who leave the company are not replaced on a 1:1 basis as long as this policy does not compromise the overall functioning of the business. Early retirement (b) is another thing companies may offer to employees who are near, but not yet at, retirement age; packages of retirement benefits that are rewarding enough can induce those who are not highly motivated to continue working other than for financial reasons to retire sooner when this is made more economically feasible. Reduced hours (c) is a strategy that can be used with those paid by the hour rather than a yearly salary; a company might change their work week from 40 to 35 hours or from 35 to 30, etc. This would address a lower work demand without firing or laying off employees. Downsizing (e) has become quite familiar in recent years and usually involves a one-time restructuring of the company in terms of its size and total number of employees.

13. B: The correct definition of outplacement is employment assistance for laid-off workers (b). Due to widespread downsizing, some firms try to mitigate the blow of being laid off by offering assistance to workers they lay off in finding work at other companies. As such, it is not the assignment of existing employees to work in other locations (c), nor is it the actual placement of employees with cooperating firms (d). It is also not a synonym for outsourcing (a), which is the practice of hiring subcontractors, often in other countries, to fulfill certain company functions. Providing for filling higher positions when they are vacated (e) is a definition of succession planning, not outplacement. Outplacement services include financial services, career guidance, teaching and tutoring related to job acquisition, personal action plan development, and ongoing support.

14. E: These are all factors that interact with T&D and affect its delivery processes (e). In addition to the support of top management, T&D also requires the involvement and commitment of all management, both generalists and specialists (a), to succeed. Giant strides in technology have provided continual advances in the way information is delivered to employees and the ways in which business is done (b), so technology has had probably the most major impact on T&D of any factor. With this progress, corporate employees are now performing more complex tasks than ever; corporate structures are more complex than ever; and the interactions between individuals and groups are also more complex (c). The increase in organizational complexity thus also affects T&D in that employees must upgrade their skills more often, adapt to more change more regularly, and use more self-direction because middle management has decreased. Fewer employees now do more work of a more complex nature. This places more demand than ever upon T&D. Another factor interacting with T&D is the fact that people have different styles of learning (d). Research finds that information must be relevant for learners to acquire it. In the business marketplace, training must be "just in time," i.e., provided on a timely basis as needed, in order to be useful to companies. Research also finds that students prefer practical and concrete orientations and activities in learning over theoretical and abstract ones and that active modes of teaching and learning are more effective than passive modes. In addition, T&D in corporations not only teaches individuals but also creates institutional knowledge on a companywide level.

15. A: Regular orientations are not designed (a) to do management development training. Management development is normally done separately, either inside or outside the company, to upgrade the skills and information needed at managerial levels. For new executives, a shortcut process known as "onboarding" is a kind of executive orientation specifically designed to help executives learn the corporate structure, corporate culture, and company politics as quickly as possible. Regular orientation for new employees who are not executives is designed to (b) acquaint them with the firm's culture; to (c) inform them of employee development programs, both inside and outside the company; to (d) integrate new workers into the company via socialization; to (e) reinforce the importance of being a team member, since this quality was likely assessed in the applicant before s/he was hired. Orientation also serves to help new workers understand how their jobs fit into the company's mission, goals and objectives, and structure; to inform new hires of corporate policies and rules; and to cover the compensation structure and process.

16. C: The T&D method least likely to involve a classroom and instructor is (c) job rotation, in which an employee learns a variety of jobs done within the company. This is done as on-the-job training for new hires and/or as an opportunity for college graduates to try out different departments of a firm to test their skills before proceeding to full-time management positions. Thus it is less likely to be done in a classroom with an instructor than at the work site. The case study method (a) often takes place in the classroom with an instructor, wherein students research a certain firm and use the information they obtain to make hypothetical decisions that should show whether they have a good understanding of that firm. Apprenticeships (b) are opportunities for students to learn about a job and a company via on-the-job training that is combined with their academic courses. Thus, this training method is more likely to involve a classroom and instructor part of the time. Internships (d) are similar; in these, students attend class part of the time and work for a company part of the time. Internships may be paid or unpaid. Research finds that college graduates who completed internships first are given higher starting salaries when hired as full-time employees than graduates without internship experience. Blended training (e), as its name implies, is using a combination of training methods. Since this could involve any number of combinations, it is more likely to include classroom instruction than any strictly on-the-job training method used alone.

17. D: Onboarding (d) is not a special training area for supervisors and employees but rather is an executive orientation designed to help new executives learn about the company as expediently as possible so they may contribute to the company as soon as possible. ESL (a) is training for employees whose second language is English. This will focus on the language most needed for the particular industry involved. In areas such as Texas with large Spanish-speaking populations, not only do Spanish-speaking employees learn English, but English-speaking employees will also learn Spanish. Ethics (b) is training in morally correct behaviors. This is not only a reaction to recent corporate scandals caused by immoral behavior in some companies; it is also pragmatic, as federal guidelines dictate that firms that had already set up such programs to avoid and identify fraud will qualify for reduced sentences if they are convicted of corporate crime. Remedial (c) training is to bring employees up to basic levels of literacy and math skills. Many people are hired after high school without having the minimum knowledge needed for the work, especially because technological progress has created so many more new jobs. Anger management (e) training is aimed at preventing both domestic and workplace violence, and verbal/emotional abuse as well. This kind of training has been adapted from psychotherapy to the workplace for its usefulness in work settings. It not only improves workplace relations, but in addition, remediating abusive behavior in the home can improve both a worker's interpersonal relationships and interactions at work, and the worker's job performance in some cases.

18. A: Benchmarking (a) is not one of the levels in the Kirkpatrick Model of training evaluation. Benchmarking is not a level in a model but a process: the process of tracking and measuring a company's internal functions (such as operations or quality control). Data on these functions are then compared to data from other firms known for success in the same functions. Companies can use these comparisons to model their own practices on those of firms more successful in the same areas. Extent of learning (b) is one level of the Kirkpatrick Model. Companies may give employees pretests before training and posttests after training to see what they have learned. Behavioral change (c) is another level of the Kirkpatrick Model. Companies should assess not only what employees have learned, but also whether they actually apply this knowledge to their on-the-job performance to change their work behavior as needed. Many firms use the 360-degree feedback method of appraisal to evaluate whether training has produced changes in behavior. Getting feedback on participant opinions (d) is also a level of the Kirkpatrick Model. Asking employees their opinions of training they have undergone will supply a facet of the total picture regarding the effectiveness of T&D. Objectives achieved (e) is the fourth of Kirkpatrick's levels. Firms may use metrics to measure whether their training programs have met any of the objectives the firms have specified. For example, if an objective was to reduce employee absenteeism, the rate of absences could be measured before and after training to see if it has been reduced.

19. B: A network career path (b) involves both vertical and horizontal movement opportunities. A dual-career path (a) allows technical specialists to increase their knowledge, contribute their specialized expertise to the company, and be rewarded without being forced to move into management positions. This kind of system is also used in higher education. Using dual-career paths enables organizations to retain valuable employees who do not want to become managers or administrators. As such, the dual-career path does not involve typical vertical movement. A lateral skill path (c), as its name suggests, involves movement from one type of work to another type within the same firm without moving upward or downward in the hierarchy. This is useful for employees who are not dissatisfied with their pay or job levels but are tired of doing the same tasks and can find new motivation learning different ones without leaving the company. Because (b) is the only correct answer, answer (d), all of these paths do, is incorrect, and answer (e), none of these paths, is also incorrect.

20. E: All of these are tools for career planning (e). Career planning begins with using self-assessment (a). Individuals planning careers need to understand themselves. This includes knowing not only what skills they have, their particular aptitudes (abilities) and interests and how these would apply to certain jobs and not to others, but also their personality type and characteristics, their typical behaviors, how they interact with others, their learning styles, what motivates them, their work habits, and so forth. Some people are talented at certain tasks but would not find a good fit at certain jobs due to the atmosphere (e.g., some people thrive on a fast pace while others hate pressure; some people are energized by being surrounded by other people while others are more comfortable working alone; some people prefer a lot of direction while others flourish when given their independence; etc.). One tool designed by Benjamin Franklin that is often used to help prospective workers evaluate themselves is (b) a strength/weakness balance sheet. This helps to pinpoint visually a person's personality assets and liabilities and relate them to various jobs. These assets and liabilities can be updated periodically because people can change over time. A likes and dislikes survey (c) is another tool that can help an individual to identify what characteristics they would like in a job and those they would dislike. Since all of these (e) is correct, none of these (d) is incorrect.

21. B: A purpose for using performance appraisal is not (or should not be) to reward or to punish an employee (b). This is more commonly a reason for either inflating or deflating an employee's performance appraisal ratings. When a supervisor does this for any of a number of reasons (e.g., to get rid of a difficult employee or one the supervisor dislikes by artificially lowering the person's ratings, or to protect a good employee undergoing personal problems or to reward an employee for effort regardless of results by artificially inflating the ratings), the true goals of performance appraisal will not be reached and the appraisal process is compromised. In addition to HR planning, recruitment and selection, and T&D choices, other legitimate reasons for using performance appraisal include as an aid to career planning or development (a); to help managers decide what kinds of pay adjustments to make (c); to help management make such internal relations decisions (d) as those regarding promotions, demotions, firing, layoffs, and transfers; and to evaluate employees' potential future performance in different jobs (e) than their current positions.

22. C: Halo error is generalizing one positive aspect of an employee's performance to all other aspects, while horn error is generalizing one negative aspect to all others. As such, the two are opposites. Therefore halo error is to horn error as (c) leniency in ratings is to strictness in ratings, because leniency results in falsely high ratings while strictness results in falsely low ratings. With halo error, one thing about the worker's performance will be rated accurately, but others not as exemplary will be inaccurately rated just as highly. With horn error, one thing about the worker's performance will get a deserved negative rating but others less negative will receive an equally negative but undeserved rating. The only difference is that with leniency or strictness, all of the ratings may be inaccurate, while with halo or horn error, at least one of the ratings will be more accurate, but the appraiser will let this color other ratings to be inaccurate by making them match the accurate (positive or negative) one. Appraiser discomfort and employee anxiety (a) are more similar than opposite as they both make the appraisal process tortuous. Lack of objectivity and recent behavior bias (b) are also not opposites. Appraisals based mainly on the employee's personal traits tend to be subjective, and it is hard to prove these traits are job related. Recent behavior bias refers to considering the employee's more recent behavior rather than longer-term behavior or behavior during specified time periods. Any kind of bias automatically renders an appraisal less objective. So these two are related but are neither opposites nor the same. Recent behavior bias and stereotyping (d) are neither opposites nor the same. Stereotyping is letting one's ratings be influenced by individual differences such as age, race or ethnicity, gender, etc. Therefore, these are both types of bias and this is mainly what they have in common. Manipulating the system (e) means the appraiser bases the employee's ratings not on objective measures and/or the appraiser's fairest possible opinions, but rather makes the ratings high or low for some ulterior motive (e.g., to keep or get rid of an employee), while personal bias (e) is another term for stereotyping [see (d) above]. Thus, these two have in common the fact that neither is an objective appraisal method, but being different instances of subjectivity, they are not the same any more than they are opposites.

23. D: The method that uses the largest number of feedback sources is (d) the 720-degree review method. This method gets feedback from multiple levels within the company, from sources outside the company, and from customers and/or investors as well. It is an extension of and beyond the 360-degree feedback evaluation method (e), which uses feedback from multiple levels within the company and from outside the company. The 720-degree method was developed by Rick Galbreath to improve on the 360-degree method by including the customer's (or investor's) perspective. The critical incident method (a) uses written records and other data and can be performed by one rater, typically the employee's supervisor or manager. The essay method (b) uses a brief narrative written by the employee's supervisor or manager and also is typically done by one rater. The forced distribution method (c) has the rater assigning members of a work group to a finite number of categories and can also be done by one rater, typically the manager in charge of that work group or team.

24. A: The BARS, or Behaviorally Anchored Rating Scale, method (a) uses specific examples of what behaviors or things an employee would do in order to meet each rating category (from Very Poor Performance at the bottom to Clearly Outstanding Performance at the top) for each ability or competence measured. This decreases rater bias and makes the appraisal less subjective because the rater can refer to these examples of observable behaviors to see which one of the descriptions the employee's actions fit most closely. The BARS method has a total of seven rating categories for each factor evaluated. Therefore, it does not have more categories (b) than rating scales, and this is not a difference, let alone being the only difference. Likewise, it does not have fewer categories (d) than rating scales. The BARS method is not simply one specific kind of rating scale with a name (c); it is rather a rating scale with behavioral anchors (the specific behavioral examples for each category or degree of below average, average, or above average performance). This makes it different from simple rating scales that have no such behavioral anchors. BARS is an acronym for Behaviorally Anchored Rating Scale and does not in any way refer to a bar graph (e), which is not used at all to depict the results of this appraisal method.

25. E: The correct definition of internal equity is (e) when employees are paid according to the relative importance or value of their jobs within the same company. When employees are paid like employees with like jobs in other firms (a), this is the definition of external equity. When those doing similar jobs in the same firm are paid differently according to individual variables (b) such as job performance, productivity rate, or seniority (length of time at the company), this is a definition of employee equity. When employees on a team or in a work group are all paid equally based on the group's achievement (c), this is a definition of team equity. A perception by firms and individuals of fairness in payment for employees (d) is a definition of financial equity.

26. C: The job evaluation method that is a variation of one of the other four is (c) the Hay Plan, or the Hay Guide Chart–Profile Method, which is a refined version of the point method (a). In the point method, numerical values are given to specified compensable elements of a job (such as education or initiative). The sum of all the numbers represents the relative value of the job. Traditionally, the point method in some form has been the most popular. The ranking method (b) is the simplest of the four. Job descriptions are ranked according to their relative worth to the company. The classification method (d) delineates different classes or grades of difficulty within each group of jobs. Raters compare job descriptions with class descriptions. The federal government's evaluation system is composed of 18 classes, which may be the most familiar example of the classification method. The factor comparison method (e) is quantitative, whereas the ranking and classification methods are qualitative. Factor comparison is also more complex than the qualitative methods. It is based on five universal factors: mental requirements; skills; physical requirements; responsibilities; and working conditions. Raters evaluate each of these factors separately. An evaluation committee devises a money-based scale. It then ranks each job by its value in terms of each of the five factors. This method produces an absolute value for each job as well as defining its relative value as the other methods do.

27. B: A bonus is a type of (b) variable pay. As more companies subscribe to the idea of pay for performance, they are setting aside more of their budgets for variable pay programs. Of a number of types of variable pay, the most common type is a one-time annual reward for being productive that is not added to an employee's base pay—i.e., a bonus. Merit pay (a) is an increase in base pay for performance over time. (It has been noted, though, that often merit pay is simply a disguised cost-of-living adjustment.) Piecework pay (c) is payment per unit produced, used in jobs involving the manufacture or assembly of concrete items. It may be the only payment, or in some cases it may be an incentive paid in addition to a guaranteed base rate. Skill-based pay (d), as its name implies, is payment for the knowledge or skills an employee possesses or acquires. For example, one employee who knows how to work more machines or how to complete more customer service processes would be paid more than another employee who knows how to work fewer machines or complete fewer processes. Competency-based pay (e) is payment for a worker's competencies, which include not only skills, but also values, attitudes, self-concepts, and motivational factors that contribute to superior job performance. Management typically defines the competencies needed for certain jobs and then prices groups of competencies.

28. A: Broadbanding (a) is the name for the practice of collapsing many salary grades into a few groups, or broad bands, containing a wide range of jobs. This makes the compensation system simpler and more flexible and saves the time of having to render very fine distinctions among specific jobs that are not that far apart. It can also encourage lateral rather than vertical movement among jobs, because employees could change to a job on the same level or even on a lower level with no change in pay. At the same time, there can be plenty of potential for salary raises within each band. Pay ranges (b) mean that a job has a range with a lowest and highest possible salary, within which the employee's payment will be. This affords the opportunity to receive pay raises within the same range based on performance and/or seniority. Wage curves (c) or pay curves refer to the practice of assuring smooth transitions from one pay grade to the next via plotting points, which when connected create either a curved line or a straight line. A single-rate system (d) or fixed-rate system dictates that every employee doing the same job gets the same base payment regardless of productivity. This is usually applied when all the jobs in a group or department are very regular in nature (such as on an assembly line) so that workers are not able to achieve widely different production rates. Adjusting pay rates (e) refers to the process required of managers when they find that some jobs are either overpaid or underpaid. Adjustment is done by either moving the job into the more appropriate pay grade for underpaid jobs and raising the pay accordingly; promoting employees to a higher pay grade in the case of overpaid jobs; making a pay cut, also in the case of overpaid jobs; or freezing the payment rate until such time as overall payment increases even out the disparity.

29. D: Payment for time not worked (d) is not a legally mandated employee benefit. It is rather termed a voluntary or discretionary benefit, i.e., the employee may choose it but it is not required by law. It can include paid vacations, paid sick leave, paid personal leave, sabbaticals, paid leave for civic duty, and others. Social Security (a) benefits are legally mandated by the Social Security Act of 1935, which was a part of Franklin D. Roosevelt's New Deal legislation. Workers' compensation (b) is also required by federal regulations and is administered individually by each state; it provides benefits to assist with the medical and other expenses of job-related injuries or illnesses. Family and medical leave (c) is legally mandated by the Family and Medical Leave Act (FMLA) of 1993. This law states that all government agencies, and private companies with at least 50 employees, give workers who have worked there for at least a year and worked at least 1,250 hours during the year right before the leave up to 12 weeks per year of unpaid leave for certain circumstances, maintaining health insurance during that leave, and giving the workers the right to return to the same or an equal job at the end of the leave period. The circumstances for this leave include pregnancy, maternity, illness, injury, and family or personal issues. Unemployment compensation (e) is legally required to be paid to workers whose positions were terminated by no fault of their own. The government's Department of Labor must pay them an amount that represents a percentage of their former wages for up to 26 weeks or until they secure new employment. This benefit is based on both federal guidelines and state statutes and, like workers' compensation, is administered separately by each state.

30. E: All of these are (e) considered discretionary, or voluntary, employee benefits; i.e., they are not required by law for an employer to provide them to its employees, but if the employer chooses to make them available, employees may elect to avail themselves of these benefits. (With some unionized jobs, the employee simply gets these benefits after a minimum length of service and cannot opt out of them but is not charged extra for them either, because they are included in the benefits package negotiated between the union and the management.) Many, but certainly not all, employers provide health insurance (a) for their employees. Group health insurance usually makes up 25% of an employee's total benefit expenses. Nearly all corporations offer group life insurance (b) to their employees to allow benefits to be paid to help the employee's family in the event of an employee's death. Retirement plans (c) are not required by law either; however, employers constitute one of the main sources of income for retirees. A retirement plan may be a defined benefit plan, which pays a fixed amount when the employee retires; or a defined contribution plan, wherein working employees regularly contribute certain amounts from their wages to a fund created for their retirement, such as a 401(k) plan, an IRA (Individual Retirement Account), a Roth IRA, or a Keogh plan. Disability plans (d) are also not required by law. Worker's compensation is a legal requirement of employers, but many employers also offer additional, more comprehensive coverage such as short-term disability and long-term disability plans. These can help employees if, for example, they have an injury or illness that is not job related. Short-term disability plans usually become effective after a company's paid sick leave expires, with long-term disability taking effect after short-term disability benefits expire.

31. D: Since OSHA was formed by the Occupational Safety and Health Act of 1970, its work has (d) reduced work mortality by more than 60% and reduced job-related injury and illness by 40%. The figures of 30% and 10% (a), 40% and 20% (b), 50% and 30% (c), respectively, for these reductions are lower than what OSHA has actually accomplished. The figures of 70% and 50%, (e), respectively for these reductions are higher. Decreasing work deaths, injuries, and illnesses by as much as OSHA has done in the past several decades is impressive considering that during that same time, the number of workers and work sites in the United States has more than doubled.

32. C: Professor (c) is not listed as one of the 12 most stressful jobs by NIOSH's ranking. Primarily, the greater degree of control over their jobs that professors enjoy, as well as the combination of salary and benefits at most (but not all) universities and colleges; the amount of education required for the job; work environment and (usually) conditions; and the nature of the work itself can account for this occupation being less stressful than many others. On the other hand, occupations ranked among the most stressful dozen include those of secretary (a), primarily due to lack of control within an office hierarchy, as well as pay that can often be low; waitress (b), due also to lack of control plus low base pay and dependence on varying tips, physical demands, time pressures, and often, poor treatment by customers; clinical lab technician (d), due to factors such as work with little or no margin for error that yet may also be routine and uninteresting, inadequate pay, work health hazards, and again, lack of control; and office manager (e), due to the amount of responsibility; number of tasks and employees to manage; lack of commensurate rewards; inadequate pay; amount of routine administrative work; number of unpleasant duties; in some cases a lack of more pleasant activities to balance the unpleasant ones; and relative lack of control from being in middle or lower management.

33. B: It is not true that (b) before OSHA almost no companies had good safety programs. In fact, although OSHA has increased the numbers of companies with such programs, there were quite a few companies with outstanding safety programs before 1970. In these companies, the executives had a strong sense of social responsibility for the health and safety of their workers, so they instituted means of assuring these, including preventing work-related accidents, injuries, and illnesses. It is true that conducting a job hazard analysis (JHA) can make a job or a task safer (a) to execute. A JHA is a process consisting of many steps. It breaks down a task or a job into smaller separate steps (like a task analysis in education). Each step is examined for potential hazards. In this way, hazards associated with a work task or a whole job can be prevented before they occur. It is true that complying with SARA, or the Superfund Amendments Reauthorization Act, Title III, would eliminate the most OSHA violations. This law stipulates that companies report hazards of the materials they use and the wastes they produce. The category incurring the most citations from OSHA is that of not having a program established for the written communication of such hazards. Compliance with SARA is not normally difficult or costly, yet many firms still overlook it. It is true that (d) involving employees in safety programs will enhance the programs. Requiring each individual worker to commit to safe practices on the job confers both a sense of responsibility and a resulting sense of accomplishment. Using a team approach makes the idea of looking out for one another a moral commitment. When workers take responsibility for their own safety, as well as following the examples of supervisors who carefully enforce and themselves follow the rules for safety, the workers develop positive attitudes and senses of ownership for safety programs. Employee participation in safety programs will make such programs stronger. It is also true that designating a safety engineer can improve the company's safety (e). A safety engineer or director provides safety training for employees and also identifies and rectifies hazardous conditions. A good safety engineer can make a substantial difference in a company's safety levels.

34. E: Progressiveness (e) is not a consequence that disciplinary action should have under the Hot Stove Rule. Progressive disciplinary action is a different approach to discipline than the Hot Stove Rule. The progressive model was formulated as a way to comply with the 1935 National Labor Relations Act (NLRA) or Wagner Act, one of FDR's New Deal programs. Progressive discipline proceeds in steps by first informing an employee of a concern to give him or her a chance to rectify it, and then taking steps of increasing severity as warranted. The supervisor follows a flow chart of questions that determine which disciplinary action is indicated (e.g., an oral warning, a written warning, suspension, or termination). On the other hand, the Hot Stove Rule does not involve a progression of steps. Its four consequences, based on an analogy with the consequences of touching a hot stove, are: (1.) Disciplinary action should occur immediately just as a hot stove burns immediately (b); (2.) There should be warning (a) that behaviors deemed unacceptable will incur punishment in the form of disciplinary action, just as the heat of a stove gives warning of being burnt as someone approaches it; (3.) Discipline should be applied consistently (c) just as a hot stove will burn anyone equally who touches it with equal pressure and duration; and (4.) Discipline is administered impersonally without being harsher or milder depending on the individual person, just as a hot stove will burn any person touching it regardless of who that person is.

35. A: The correct chronological order of these laws is (a): The Civil Rights Act; the Equal Pay Act; the Age Discrimination in Employment Act; the Pregnancy Discrimination Act; the Americans with Disabilities Act. The original Civil Rights Act was first passed in 1866. (There was also a Civil Rights Act of 1964, Title VII of which was amended in 1972, and a Civil Rights Act of 1991.) The Equal Pay Act, which prohibits unequal pay based on gender for doing the same job, was passed in 1963. The Age Discrimination in Employment Act was passed in 1967 to ban discrimination against those aged 40 to 65 years. (It was amended in 1978 to include those between 40 and 70 years of age, and again in 1986 to include all those aged 40 or older, reflecting increased life spans in American society as well as economic considerations leading to many people working longer.) The Pregnancy Discrimination Act was passed in 1978. The Americans with Disabilities Act (ADA) was passed in 1990.

36. C: The Civil Rights Act of 1991 did not amend the Immigration Reform and Control Act (c) of 1986. It did amend Title VII of the 1964 Civil Rights Act (a); the Rehabilitation Act (b) of 1973; the Age Discrimination in Employment Act (d) of 1967; and the Americans with Disabilities Act (e) of 1990. This legislation was made by Congress to overturn six Supreme Court rulings made in 1988 and 1989 regarding employment discrimination.

37. B: The first law to address minimum wages was (b) the Davis-Bacon Act of 1931. This law dictates a prevailing wage, set at the union wage by the Secretary of Labor, for all construction projects receiving federal funding or assistance of more than $2,000.00. The Walsh-Healy Act (a) of 1936 stipulates that firms having contracts with the federal government for supplies for more than $10,000.00 must pay prevailing wages. The Walsh-Healy Act of 1936 also set the minimum overtime pay for working more than 8 hours a day or 40 hours a week at time-and-a-half. The Fair Labor Standards Act (c) of 1938 (FLSA) was the law to set a minimum wage. It also set standards for child labor and requirements for keeping records, among other things. The Equal Pay Act (d) of 1963 prohibited unequal pay for the same job on the basis of gender. The Civil Rights Act (e) of 1866 prohibited employment discrimination based on race. The Civil Rights Act of 1964 and the amendment of its Title VII by the Equal Employment Act of 1972 expanded the law to prohibit employment discrimination based on sex, religion, national origin, or color and to prohibit retaliation against an employee for participating in a hearing, investigation, or proceeding. The Civil Rights Act of 1991 amended both previous Civil Rights Acts and the latter's amendment, as well as three other laws to address certain Supreme Court decisions and to address disparate impact on protected groups.

38. D: Inside sales (d) employees are not considered exempt from overtime provisions according to FLSA. These are employees whose job duties include making sales to customers, but they do this at the job site (for example, over the telephone). On the other hand, outside salespersons (e) are considered exempt employees; they do their selling outside of the workplace (for example, by visiting customers' places of business). Executives (a) such as managers; administrators (b) who are not managers but perform significant functions, such as registrars, bursars, account executives, or market researchers; and professionals (c) such as doctors, lawyers, or statisticians working for a company, are all typically classified as exempt employees.

39. A: HIPAA (a), or the Health Insurance Portability and Accountability Act (1996), includes protection of self-employed individuals, people with pre-existing medical conditions, and privacy of personal health information. The main aim of this law is to make health insurance continuous for workers and to allow it to be portable across jobs. COBRA (b) is the Consolidated Omnibus Budget Reconciliation Act (1985). This law allows employees to retain the employer-provided group health insurance for themselves and their families for up to 18 months after termination of their employment. ERISA (c), the Employee Retirement Income Security Act (1974), protects retiring employees by giving greater assurance that those who have participated in a retirement plan will actually have access to the retirement income they deserve when they retire. Due to mismanagement of retirement funds, this often did not occur, and this legislation was a response to that problem. OWBPA (d) stands for the Older Workers Benefit Protection Act (1990), which is an amendment to the Age Discrimination in Employment Act; it prevents age-based discrimination in administering benefits and also allows voluntary early retirement incentive plans. The PPA (e) is the Pension Protection Act (2006), which reinforces the rules for funding defined-benefit pension plans. This law aims to see that companies make larger contributions to their pension funds rather than "dumping" them on the federal insuring company, the Pension Benefit Guaranty Corporation (PBGC), as some major corporations had done, creating a deficit of billions of dollars for that entity. The law raises the liabilities for "at-risk" pension plans and also facilitates automatic enrollment of employees in companies' 401(k) plans.

40. E: OSHA does not include the condition that (e) harm is not imminent but the worker would rather wait for a resolution of the potentially harmful problem before working again. According to OSHA, it is legal for a worker to refuse to work under these conditions: (a) the worker has a reasonable fear of death, illness, or serious physical injury; (b) harm to the worker is imminent, i.e., likely to happen right away or soon; (c) enough time does not exist to file a complaint to OSHA and have the problem fixed; (d) the worker has informed the employer and asked for a resolution of the problem that could cause harm, but the employer has not responded to this request.

41. A: Characteristics identified by the National Safe Workplace Institute of businesses at high risk for workplace violence do not include (a) frequent use of dangerous or potentially hazardous machinery. This could increase a company's risk for workplace injuries, but not for violence by employees. Frequent grievance filing by employees (b) is a characteristic, as the more dissatisfied workers are, the more they are likely to complain, and if their complaints are not resolved satisfactorily, there is potential for their anger to escalate. Similarly, if labor and management are often at odds, it is a sign that both may be unhappy with workplace conditions, and formal disputes may be accompanied by informal verbal arguments, which can escalate into physical actions at times. If workers often file claims for workers' compensation, and particularly for psychological harm (d), this is another sign that workers feel they are mistreated in the workplace; if this situation continues unresolved, some workers could retaliate with violence. If management in a business often insists on overtime work (as opposed to workers voluntarily working overtime for the added income) and this is combined with understaffing (e), there is more potential for workers to rebel.

42. D: Workers suffering from a major mental illness (d) have certainly been a reason behind some cases of workplace violence; however, this is not one of the most common reasons for violence against a company by workers or former workers. These cases can seem more prevalent than they are when the violence is extreme (e.g., shootings causing multiple deaths) and the episodes receive so much publicity in the media. However, other cases of equal violence have been committed by people without diagnosed mental illness who apparently are sane but are seriously disgruntled. (For example, on December 26, 2000, in Wakefield, Massachusetts, Michael McDermott, age 42, a software programmer at Edgewater Technology, shot and killed five other employees because the company's accounting department had garnished his salary to pay the IRS his overdue income tax.) The most frequent reasons for workplace violence include firings and/or layoffs made by the company (a); problems an employee is experiencing in his/her marriage or family (b); substance abuse problems an employee is experiencing (c); and differences between an employee and supervisor(s) or coworker(s) arising from personality conflicts (e).

43. B: A bank teller working the day shift with a full staff (b) is at relatively less risk of being a victim of workplace violence than the others listed. It is found by NIOSH that 90% of these other types of workers listed are victims of armed criminals rather than of angry coworkers. While working with money and working with the public are risk factors for the bank teller, the facts that the teller is working in the daytime and is surrounded by many coworkers mitigate the risk. Working in a liquor store and working alone (a) are major risk factors for being attacked by armed criminals. Drivers of taxi cabs (c) and delivery drivers (d) are 60 times more likely than other employees to be killed while working. The fact that the cab driver also works in a city is an additional danger because urban areas tend to have higher crime rates. NIOSH has also identified police officers working the night shift (e) as one of the groups of employees in the greatest danger of violence on the job. (Being armed themselves and being trained in police techniques do not afford greater protection, as these are balanced out by the fact that officers come into much more contact with criminals and other individuals with violent behavior who are also armed.)

44. E: It is true that the Fair and Accurate Credit Transactions Act (FACTA) concentrates on information used to determine qualification for employment, for credit, for insurance, and other uses (e). It is not true that the law making identity theft a federal crime was passed in 2000 (a); this law, the Identity Theft and Assumption Deterrence Act, was passed by Congress in 1988. It is not true that FACTA requires sensitive consumer information to be destroyed (b). FACTA was passed in

2003, but the legislation actually requiring both companies and individuals to dispose appropriately of sensitive consumer information was the Federal Trade Commission's (FTC's) Disposal Rule, which became effective in 2005. It is not true that identity theft is no longer a problem because these pieces of legislation have passed (c); despite these measures, identity theft remains an issue, both for individuals and in the workplace. It is also not true that FACTA was passed as a response to the FTC's Disposal Rule (d); it is the opposite—the Disposal Rule was made in 2005 as a response to the passage of FACTA in 2003.

45. C: The correct statement is that (c) the Landrum-Griffin Act allows closed shops in the construction industry. It is only in the construction industry that a closed shop is allowed. A closed shop is a union practice that requires union membership of any employee in order to be hired. The closed shop practice was not legalized by the Taft-Hartley Act (a); the Taft-Hartley Act, or the Labor-Management Relations Act, passed in 1947, made the closed shop uniformly illegal. The Landrum-Griffin Act did not simply legalize the closed shop (b). In 1959, this law legalized a closed shop ONLY for the construction business. There are no other exceptions to the Taft-Hartley Act's ban of closed shops except for in construction. Thus it is not the Taft-Hartley Act that allows closed shops for construction companies (d) but the Landrum-Griffin Act. And it is therefore not true that the Landrum-Griffin Act made closed shops illegal (e); this was done by the Taft-Hartley Act.

46. E: Conducting a lockout (e) is a strategy management can use if collective bargaining negotiations between a labor union and management break down. A lockout refers to management actually locking employees out of the building or work site. Operations are continued using management staff and/or replacement staff (such as nonunion employees or temporary workers). This technique is often effective as union workers receive no pay during a lockout, and it is particularly so if the union is not strong and/or money is scarce. Strikes (a) are a strategy used by unions in the face of negotiation breakdowns during collective bargaining. Union workers walk out and refuse to work until their demands are met. Boycotts (b) are also a strategy used by unions if negotiations break down. Union workers agree they will not buy or use the company's products. This is effective by putting economic pressure on the company's management. It has longer-lasting effects than strikes do, as changes in buying behaviors are apt to go on after the end of the boycott. Informational picketing (c) is a union strategy used to garner public support for the union members' cause. While it may appear to some people to resemble a strike, it is not the same; union workers typically exhibit signs or posters and distribute pamphlets or leaflets with information they want the public to know. However, the informational picketing done by some union members does not mean that all union members are refusing to work, as in a strike. Secondary boycotts (d) are illegal according to the Taft-Hartley Act (1947). However, some unions have tried to use them regardless. A secondary boycott is a union tactic wherein members try to convince third parties, such as customers of the business or vendors of supplies to the business, to boycott the company's products as well as the union members themselves doing so.

47. D: The most common type of employees by far in global staffs is (d) host-country national employees. These are employees who are citizens of the country where the corporation's branch or subsidiary is located; for example, a Dutch citizen working in Holland for an American corporation's Dutch branch would be a host-country national. Host-country nationals make up more than 98% of foreign operations employees in North American and Western European multinational corporations in the majority of industries. Third-country nationals (a) are employees who are citizens of one country working in another country for a company that has its headquarters in a third country. For example, a citizen of France who works in England for a Japanese company would be a third-country national type of employee. Expatriates (b) are employees who are citizens of the country where the company's headquarters are located, but not of the country where the company's operations take place. For example, if a French corporate headquarters assigns an employee who is a French citizen to work in the firm's Italian plant, this employee would be an expatriate. Since (d) is the most common type, (c), none of these is most common, is incorrect, and (e), stating that (a) and (b) are both most common, is also incorrect.

48. C: Ethnocentric staffing (c) is the kind of global staffing wherein mainly expatriates are hired as upper management in foreign locations. This practice is based on the belief that expatriates will emphasize home office perspectives above those of local perspectives and assure a good connection between foreign operations and their parent companies. Geocentric staffing (a) is the practice of using an integrated business strategy with worldwide application. In other words, a company tries to hire the best candidate for a position regardless of the candidate's country of origin. This approach is the most commonly used in the most global companies. It also makes corporate human resources the most complex. Polycentric staffing (b) is the practice of hiring host-country nationals companywide, from the top to the bottom of the organization. This is based on the belief that locals can more easily address local business market conditions and are more familiar with local laws, politics, culture, and business practices. It also has the advantage of communicating to the foreign base that the corporation is not simply establishing a foreign operation but also has a commitment to the host country. Regiocentric staffing (d) is the practice of having regional groups of foreign subsidiaries or branches that function together as a unit. Decisions are made with some regional autonomy, and specific sets of practices in employment develop that become common within each of the regions. Since only (c) is correct, answer (e), all of these kinds do [hire mainly expatriates], is incorrect.

49. B: A good HRIS should not be (b) complex. Managers need a system that is concise (c) because they can only take in so much information at a time, and one that is relevant (d), meaning they only get the information they need for a given circumstance. Complexity in the HRIS could mean they get too much information, which is more than they can use, which would negate conciseness and relevance. However, a good HRIS should certainly be accurate (a); managers need to receive information they can count on to be correct. It should also be complete (e); managers should never be given partial information by the system because this can distort the manager's perception of the situation.

50. A: It is not projected that workers will outnumber jobs by 2013 (a). In fact, the Department of Labor projects that by 2013, the number of jobs available will outnumber workers by 6.7 million, and by 30 million by the year 2030. It has been projected by the Bureau of Labor Statistics that the median (middle) age of workers will be above 40 years by 2010. (Even in the year 2010, it will take a few more years before data are gathered and the figures compiled for us to know whether this projection was accurate or not; statistics such as labor and census figures typically run several years behind the current year because real-time numbers cannot be known immediately.) The Bureau of Labor Statistics has also estimated that women will comprise 48% of the total workforce in 2010 (c) and that they will make up 59% of new workers entering the labor force in 2010 (d) as well. Additionally, it is estimated that more than 70 million baby boomers will be 65 years old by around the year 2023 (i.e., within around 15 years of a 2008 estimate). Contrasted with these 70 million approaching retirement age, it is projected that only 40 million new employees will come into the workforce; hence the number of jobs available will outnumber the workers available.

How to Overcome Test Anxiety

Just the thought of taking a test is enough to make most people a little nervous. A test is an important event that can have a long-term impact on your future, so it's important to take it seriously and it's natural to feel anxious about performing well. But just because anxiety is normal, that doesn't mean that it's helpful in test taking, or that you should simply accept it as part of your life. Anxiety can have a variety of effects. These effects can be mild, like making you feel slightly nervous, or severe, like blocking your ability to focus or remember even a simple detail.

If you experience test anxiety—whether severe or mild—it's important to know how to beat it. To discover this, first you need to understand what causes test anxiety.

Causes of Test Anxiety

While we often think of anxiety as an uncontrollable emotional state, it can actually be caused by simple, practical things. One of the most common causes of test anxiety is that a person does not feel adequately prepared for their test. This feeling can be the result of many different issues such as poor study habits or lack of organization, but the most common culprit is time management. Starting to study too late, failing to organize your study time to cover all of the material, or being distracted while you study will mean that you're not well prepared for the test. This may lead to cramming the night before, which will cause you to be physically and mentally exhausted for the test. Poor time management also contributes to feelings of stress, fear, and hopelessness as you realize you are not well prepared but don't know what to do about it.

Other times, test anxiety is not related to your preparation for the test but comes from unresolved fear. This may be a past failure on a test, or poor performance on tests in general. It may come from comparing yourself to others who seem to be performing better or from the stress of living up to expectations. Anxiety may be driven by fears of the future—how failure on this test would affect your educational and career goals. These fears are often completely irrational, but they can still negatively impact your test performance.

Elements of Test Anxiety

As mentioned earlier, test anxiety is considered to be an emotional state, but it has physical and mental components as well. Sometimes you may not even realize that you are suffering from test anxiety until you notice the physical symptoms. These can include trembling hands, rapid heartbeat, sweating, nausea, and tense muscles. Extreme anxiety may lead to fainting or vomiting. Obviously, any of these symptoms can have a negative impact on testing. It is important to recognize them as soon as they begin to occur so that you can address the problem before it damages your performance.

The mental components of test anxiety include trouble focusing and inability to remember learned information. During a test, your mind is on high alert, which can help you recall information and stay focused for an extended period of time. However, anxiety interferes with your mind's natural processes, causing you to blank out, even on the questions you know well. The strain of testing during anxiety makes it difficult to stay focused, especially on a test that may take several hours. Extreme anxiety can take a huge mental toll, making it difficult not only to recall test information but even to understand the test questions or pull your thoughts together.

Effects of Test Anxiety

Test anxiety is like a disease—if left untreated, it will get progressively worse. Anxiety leads to poor performance, and this reinforces the feelings of fear and failure, which in turn lead to poor performances on subsequent tests. It can grow from a mild nervousness to a crippling condition. If allowed to progress, test anxiety can have a big impact on your schooling, and consequently on your future.

Test anxiety can spread to other parts of your life. Anxiety on tests can become anxiety in any stressful situation, and blanking on a test can turn into panicking in a job situation. But fortunately, you don't have to let anxiety rule your testing and determine your grades. There are a number of relatively simple steps you can take to move past anxiety and function normally on a test and in the rest of life.

Physical Steps for Beating Test Anxiety

While test anxiety is a serious problem, the good news is that it can be overcome. It doesn't have to control your ability to think and remember information. While it may take time, you can begin taking steps today to beat anxiety.

Just as your first hint that you may be struggling with anxiety comes from the physical symptoms, the first step to treating it is also physical. Rest is crucial for having a clear, strong mind. If you are tired, it is much easier to give in to anxiety. But if you establish good sleep habits, your body and mind will be ready to perform optimally, without the strain of exhaustion. Additionally, sleeping well helps you to retain information better, so you're more likely to recall the answers when you see the test questions.

Getting good sleep means more than going to bed on time. It's important to allow your brain time to relax. Take study breaks from time to time so it doesn't get overworked, and don't study right before bed. Take time to rest your mind before trying to rest your body, or you may find it difficult to fall asleep.

Along with sleep, other aspects of physical health are important in preparing for a test. Good nutrition is vital for good brain function. Sugary foods and drinks may give a burst of energy but this burst is followed by a crash, both physically and emotionally. Instead, fuel your body with protein and vitamin-rich foods.

Also, drink plenty of water. Dehydration can lead to headaches and exhaustion, especially if your brain is already under stress from the rigors of the test. Particularly if your test is a long one, drink water during the breaks. And if possible, take an energy-boosting snack to eat between sections.

Along with sleep and diet, a third important part of physical health is exercise. Maintaining a steady workout schedule is helpful, but even taking 5-minute study breaks to walk can help get your blood pumping faster and clear your head. Exercise also releases endorphins, which contribute to a positive feeling and can help combat test anxiety.

When you nurture your physical health, you are also contributing to your mental health. If your body is healthy, your mind is much more likely to be healthy as well. So take time to rest, nourish your body with healthy food and water, and get moving as much as possible. Taking these physical steps will make you stronger and more able to take the mental steps necessary to overcome test anxiety.

Mental Steps for Beating Test Anxiety

Working on the mental side of test anxiety can be more challenging, but as with the physical side, there are clear steps you can take to overcome it. As mentioned earlier, test anxiety often stems from lack of preparation, so the obvious solution is to prepare for the test. Effective studying may be the most important weapon you have for beating test anxiety, but you can and should employ several other mental tools to combat fear.

First, boost your confidence by reminding yourself of past success—tests or projects that you aced. If you're putting as much effort into preparing for this test as you did for those, there's no reason you should expect to fail here. Work hard to prepare; then trust your preparation.

Second, surround yourself with encouraging people. It can be helpful to find a study group, but be sure that the people you're around will encourage a positive attitude. If you spend time with others who are anxious or cynical, this will only contribute to your own anxiety. Look for others who are motivated to study hard from a desire to succeed, not from a fear of failure.

Third, reward yourself. A test is physically and mentally tiring, even without anxiety, and it can be helpful to have something to look forward to. Plan an activity following the test, regardless of the outcome, such as going to a movie or getting ice cream.

When you are taking the test, if you find yourself beginning to feel anxious, remind yourself that you know the material. Visualize successfully completing the test. Then take a few deep, relaxing breaths and return to it. Work through the questions carefully but with confidence, knowing that you are capable of succeeding.

Developing a healthy mental approach to test taking will also aid in other areas of life. Test anxiety affects more than just the actual test—it can be damaging to your mental health and even contribute to depression. It's important to beat test anxiety before it becomes a problem for more than testing.

Study Strategy

Being prepared for the test is necessary to combat anxiety, but what does being prepared look like? You may study for hours on end and still not feel prepared. What you need is a strategy for test prep. The next few pages outline our recommended steps to help you plan out and conquer the challenge of preparation.

Step 1: Scope Out the Test

Learn everything you can about the format (multiple choice, essay, etc.) and what will be on the test. Gather any study materials, course outlines, or sample exams that may be available. Not only will this help you to prepare, but knowing what to expect can help to alleviate test anxiety.

Step 2: Map Out the Material

Look through the textbook or study guide and make note of how many chapters or sections it has. Then divide these over the time you have. For example, if a book has 15 chapters and you have five days to study, you need to cover three chapters each day. Even better, if you have the time, leave an extra day at the end for overall review after you have gone through the material in depth.

If time is limited, you may need to prioritize the material. Look through it and make note of which sections you think you already have a good grasp on, and which need review. While you are studying, skim quickly through the familiar sections and take more time on the challenging parts.

Write out your plan so you don't get lost as you go. Having a written plan also helps you feel more in control of the study, so anxiety is less likely to arise from feeling overwhelmed at the amount to cover.

Step 3: Gather Your Tools

Decide what study method works best for you. Do you prefer to highlight in the book as you study and then go back over the highlighted portions? Or do you type out notes of the important information? Or is it helpful to make flashcards that you can carry with you? Assemble the pens, index cards, highlighters, post-it notes, and any other materials you may need so you won't be distracted by getting up to find things while you study.

If you're having a hard time retaining the information or organizing your notes, experiment with different methods. For example, try color-coding by subject with colored pens, highlighters, or post-it notes. If you learn better by hearing, try recording yourself reading your notes so you can listen while in the car, working out, or simply sitting at your desk. Ask a friend to quiz you from your flashcards, or try teaching someone the material to solidify it in your mind.

Step 4: Create Your Environment

It's important to avoid distractions while you study. This includes both the obvious distractions like visitors and the subtle distractions like an uncomfortable chair (or a too-comfortable couch that makes you want to fall asleep). Set up the best study environment possible: good lighting and a comfortable work area. If background music helps you focus, you may want to turn it on, but otherwise keep the room quiet. If you are using a computer to take notes, be sure you don't have any other windows open, especially applications like social media, games, or anything else that could distract you. Silence your phone and turn off notifications. Be sure to keep water close by so you stay hydrated while you study (but avoid unhealthy drinks and snacks).

Also, take into account the best time of day to study. Are you freshest first thing in the morning? Try to set aside some time then to work through the material. Is your mind clearer in the afternoon or evening? Schedule your study session then. Another method is to study at the same time of day that you will take the test, so that your brain gets used to working on the material at that time and will be ready to focus at test time.

Step 5: Study!

Once you have done all the study preparation, it's time to settle into the actual studying. Sit down, take a few moments to settle your mind so you can focus, and begin to follow your study plan. Don't give in to distractions or let yourself procrastinate. This is your time to prepare so you'll be ready to fearlessly approach the test. Make the most of the time and stay focused.

Of course, you don't want to burn out. If you study too long you may find that you're not retaining the information very well. Take regular study breaks. For example, taking five minutes out of every hour to walk briskly, breathing deeply and swinging your arms, can help your mind stay fresh.

As you get to the end of each chapter or section, it's a good idea to do a quick review. Remind yourself of what you learned and work on any difficult parts. When you feel that you've mastered the material, move on to the next part. At the end of your study session, briefly skim through your notes again.

But while review is helpful, cramming last minute is NOT. If at all possible, work ahead so that you won't need to fit all your study into the last day. Cramming overloads your brain with more information than it can process and retain, and your tired mind may struggle to recall even previously learned information when it is overwhelmed with last-minute study. Also, the urgent nature of cramming and the stress placed on your brain contribute to anxiety. You'll be more likely to go to the test feeling unprepared and having trouble thinking clearly.

So don't cram, and don't stay up late before the test, even just to review your notes at a leisurely pace. Your brain needs rest more than it needs to go over the information again. In fact, plan to finish your studies by noon or early afternoon the day before the test. Give your brain the rest of the day to relax or focus on other things, and get a good night's sleep. Then you will be fresh for the test and better able to recall what you've studied.

Step 6: Take a Practice Test

Many courses offer sample tests, either online or in the study materials. This is an excellent resource to check whether you have mastered the material, as well as to prepare for the test format and environment.

Check the test format ahead of time: the number of questions, the type (multiple choice, free response, etc.), and the time limit. Then create a plan for working through them. For example, if you have 30 minutes to take a 60-question test, your limit is 30 seconds per question. Spend less time on the questions you know well so that you can take more time on the difficult ones.

If you have time to take several practice tests, take the first one open book, with no time limit. Work through the questions at your own pace and make sure you fully understand them. Gradually work up to taking a test under test conditions: sit at a desk with all study materials put away and set a timer. Pace yourself to make sure you finish the test with time to spare and go back to check your answers if you have time.

After each test, check your answers. On the questions you missed, be sure you understand why you missed them. Did you misread the question (tests can use tricky wording)? Did you forget the information? Or was it something you hadn't learned? Go back and study any shaky areas that the practice tests reveal.

Taking these tests not only helps with your grade, but also aids in combating test anxiety. If you're already used to the test conditions, you're less likely to worry about it, and working through tests until you're scoring well gives you a confidence boost. Go through the practice tests until you feel comfortable, and then you can go into the test knowing that you're ready for it.

Test Tips

On test day, you should be confident, knowing that you've prepared well and are ready to answer the questions. But aside from preparation, there are several test day strategies you can employ to maximize your performance.

First, as stated before, get a good night's sleep the night before the test (and for several nights before that, if possible). Go into the test with a fresh, alert mind rather than staying up late to study.

Try not to change too much about your normal routine on the day of the test. It's important to eat a nutritious breakfast, but if you normally don't eat breakfast at all, consider eating just a protein bar. If you're a coffee drinker, go ahead and have your normal coffee. Just make sure you time it so that the caffeine doesn't wear off right in the middle of your test. Avoid sugary beverages, and drink enough water to stay hydrated but not so much that you need a restroom break 10 minutes into the test. If your test isn't first thing in the morning, consider going for a walk or doing a light workout before the test to get your blood flowing.

Allow yourself enough time to get ready, and leave for the test with plenty of time to spare so you won't have the anxiety of scrambling to arrive in time. Another reason to be early is to select a good seat. It's helpful to sit away from doors and windows, which can be distracting. Find a good seat, get out your supplies, and settle your mind before the test begins.

When the test begins, start by going over the instructions carefully, even if you already know what to expect. Make sure you avoid any careless mistakes by following the directions.

Then begin working through the questions, pacing yourself as you've practiced. If you're not sure on an answer, don't spend too much time on it, and don't let it shake your confidence. Either skip it and come back later, or eliminate as many wrong answers as possible and guess among the remaining ones. Don't dwell on these questions as you continue—put them out of your mind and focus on what lies ahead.

Be sure to read all of the answer choices, even if you're sure the first one is the right answer. Sometimes you'll find a better one if you keep reading. But don't second-guess yourself if you do immediately know the answer. Your gut instinct is usually right. Don't let test anxiety rob you of the information you know.

If you have time at the end of the test (and if the test format allows), go back and review your answers. Be cautious about changing any, since your first instinct tends to be correct, but make sure you didn't misread any of the questions or accidentally mark the wrong answer choice. Look over any you skipped and make an educated guess.

At the end, leave the test feeling confident. You've done your best, so don't waste time worrying about your performance or wishing you could change anything. Instead, celebrate the successful completion of this test. And finally, use this test to learn how to deal with anxiety even better next time.

Review Video: Test Anxiety
Visit mometrix.com/academy and enter code: 100340

Important Qualification

Not all anxiety is created equal. If your test anxiety is causing major issues in your life beyond the classroom or testing center, or if you are experiencing troubling physical symptoms related to your anxiety, it may be a sign of a serious physiological or psychological condition. If this sounds like your situation, we strongly encourage you to seek professional help.

Online Resources

Due to our efforts to try to keep this book to a manageable length, we've created a link that will give you access to all of your online resources:

mometrix.com/resources719/dssthumresman

It's Your Moment, Let's Celebrate It!

Share your story @mometrixtestpreparation